Come Let Us Adore

St. Gregory's Abbey, 1999-2011

Articles and Photographs by
the Monks of St. Gregory's Abbey

Edited by Andrew Marr, OSB

iUniverse, Inc.
Bloomington

Come Let Us Adore
St. Gregory's Abbey, 1999-2011

iUniverse books may be ordered through booksellers or by contacting:

iUniverse
1663 Liberty Drive
Bloomington, IN 47403
www.iuniverse.com
1-800-Authors (1-800-288-4677)

ISBN: 978-1-4620-3045-3 (sc)
ISBN: 978-1-4620-3046-0 (e)

Printed in the United States of America

iUniverse rev. date: 06/30/2011

Table of Contents

Introduction
By Abbot Andrew Marr

I start a typical day by entering the abbey church at four in the morning, my head still fogged with sleep, to say Matins. (On Sundays and major feasts, we sleep in to five-thirty.) Before I joined the monastery, I had heard that the human body is at its weakest between roughly two and four in the morning. My experience of getting up at that hour to pray has convinced me that this is true. And yet I feel that there is great value in praying at an hour when I am weak because, in my weakness, God prays through me with greater freedom than later in the day when I have more energy.

Matins opens with Psalm Three and then moves to an invitation to prayer we call the Invitatory: Psalm 95 plus an antiphon, a verse that serves as a refrain. Psalm 95 starts out as a hymn of praise: "O come ring our joy to the Lord; hail the rock who saves us," but moves on to warn us not to grumble as did the Israelites in the desert at Meribah, a salutary warning for any community.

Many of the antiphons for festive occasions include the phrase: "Come let us adore." At the beginning of Advent, the antiphon is "The Lord the king who is to come * Come let us adore." Starting with the third Sunday in Advent, the antiphon changes to "Now the Lord is near * Come let us adore." When Christmas comes, we say: "Christ is born for us * Come let us adore," and then for Epiphany the antiphon becomes: "Christ has appeared to us * Come let us adore."

Some antiphons for saints' days also use this verse, such as the antiphon for the feast of an apostle: "The Lord, king of apostles * Come let us adore." For John the Baptist, we say: "Lamb of God foretold by John * Come let us adore."

Normal week day antiphons are key verses from Psalm 95 so it isn't all that often that we have "come let us adore" antiphons, but they are numerous enough to set the tone of the office for me. Whether we use this particular refrain on a given morning or not, coming to adore Christ is what our life at the abbey is all about.

Coming to adore Christ first thing in the morning is what we were doing at St. Gregory's Abbey throughout our first sixty years covered in *Singing God's Praises* and it has continued to be what we have been doing in the twelve years covered by this book. No news there. Just the same old thing, day in and day out. But doing the same old thing day in and day out is par for the course in Benedictine monasticism. For a Benedictine monastery, it is closer to the norm than the exception to have a dozen years or so with nothing new to report.

And yet, there is a news item to report. We have completed the building program that had been going off and on since 1988. I remember, back when we started, recalling that many monastic building projects have taken decades to complete. I hoped, in vain as it turned out, that it wouldn't be so with us. Even so, twenty years for a major building project is faster than some monastic projects have taken. I have learned through all this that sometimes we have to learn to be patient whether we like it or not. In the end, our patience was rewarded. Now, the community and our guests eat in a new dining hall and our books are housed in a new library which has proved to be infinitely more comfortable and convenient for all readers. Our building project was completed in 2009 when we built a great hall that connects the dining hall and library to the church. The old farm house that was replaced is shown above and the new building that replaced it is shown below. A bell tower is now the focal point of our layout. The great hall makes a perfect space for the blessings of the palms on Palm Sunday and the lighting of the Paschal candle at the start of the Easter vigil.

This exterior makeover has enhanced our sense of well-being in many ways, but it has not changed our monastic life interiorly. We still have the same group of life-professed monks we did when we published *Singing God's Praises*, though we were graced with the presence of Br. Cuthbert for over five years before he came to the conclusion that he was not called to a life-long monastic vocation. During these past years, we have continued our practice of publishing the *Abbey Letter* with a feature article in each issue. The only change here is that Br. Abraham has taken over the duty of producing it, relieving Fr. Jude who did the job so well for over thirty-five years. I think these articles show that although we keep on doing the same old things, we keep seeing the same old things anew. Praying the Divine Office and reading scripture daily challenges us to think and pray and think and pray again about what our lives are all about. In this book, we offer a generous selection of articles published over these last twelve years. They are now conveniently available to read again and again while reflecting on the words that have come out of our reflections. As often happens in a collection such as this, some of the same points come up in differing contexts, leading to some repetitiveness. Even so, these repetitions lead to differing nuances of insight. In any case, these articles are designed to be read one at a time for maximum effect.

We are still waiting on God to send us more vocations to sustain the life of St. Gregory's well into the future. We have a postulant at this time, and that is a start. I think we can take some encouragement that waiting for the building program's completion led to the monastic buildings we have now. It is up to those of us committed to life in this monastery to continue building the house inside the heart of God for the sake of all who benefit from our ministry of prayer.

Prologue:
Easter-Summer-Fall-Christmas
By Fr. Jude

From the Easter 2002 Abbey Letter

The monks of St. Gregory's Abbey have been publishing their small magazine under the name *Abbey Letter* since 1969, having changed to that name from *Benedicite* at the same time that English replaced Latin as the language of worship in the abbey church. The four issues of the Abbey Letter published in the course of a year were labeled Spring, Summer, Fall, and Winter, an easy, sensible scheme. However, the Abbey Letters mailed out in December of 1973 said "Christmas 1973" on the cover. The following issue read "Easter 1974." But there was no change in the first part of the date on the next two issues; they remained "Summer" and "Fall." And the yearly sequence is still Easter-Summer-Fall- Christmas, not quite logical, a bit odd.

I had joined the community in

5

December of 1971, and I don't remember that there was any discussion in 1973 about changing "Winter" to "Christmas" and "Spring" to "Easter." Although I don't know why the dating scheme was changed, it seems to me that it was a good idea. Besides adding a note of mild eccentricity, a traditional monastic trait, the sequence expresses something about the relationship of time and eternity, about God's time and our time. That is, two historical (datable, in principle) events crucial to us Christians and, we believe, to all creation, receive mention in the titling of two of the four issues of the year, coexisting with two expressions of repetitious cyclical time in the names of two seasons of the year.

Each year, we are concerned about getting the *Abbey Letter* to our readers before Easter, but not too long before. Even though Easter's date moves from year to year with the wandering moon, it has a definite place in earth's own calendar. Sometimes it wanders too far for convenience; there was one year when the Abbey Letter mailed in spring said Eastertide because we could not manage to get it out by that year's early Easter. The summer and fall issues are easier to schedule. We allow ourselves a couple of weeks leeway in getting those into the mail. [*Recent postal regulations require sending the Abbey Letter out at precise intervals four times a year, so the mailings now occur at fixed times rather than varying with the dating of Easter. Ed.*]

I come across the opinion here and there that the Resurrection took place out of time and should not be thought of as a historical event. Certainly God's own metatemporal eternity was involved, but his Time touched and invaded our earthly time most wonderfully. The Resurrection is a real event in our earth's history, an event which overarches all our days, past, present, and future. Jesus' resurrection culminates the earthly life which began with the day for which our Christmas Abbey Letter is named. I haven't heard anyone suggest that our Lord's birth did not take place within time. We would not insist on December 25, but we are certain that Jesus does have an earth- time birthday.

Something that did not take place in time, though, was God's first gift to us, that gift without which other gifts could have no being: Creation. It didn't take place in time; it was the beginning of time. For the time of this earth the daily round of light and dark, the changing phases of the moon, the procession of the seasons is inherent in God's creation of the world, and was established from the beginning. So we don't have an anniversary on which to celebrate creation. But God's act of creation must not be forgotten nor our thanks for it omitted. For God's creative love is the basis of our being, here and now, the power by which you and I exist. For that love we give him glory.

We monks have an advantage here; early every Sunday at Lauds we offer in praise the great hymn of Creation *Benedicite omnia opera Domini* (see page 88 in the Book of Common Prayer). Both the Daily Office in the Book of Common Prayer and the seven-fold monastic office that we pray here at St. Gregory's are offered in response to God's gift of being, both to ourselves and to the whole creation. The returning day by day, even hour by hour, to the praise of God the Creator is an imitation of God's own constancy and faithfulness in providing the arena where his saving work rains blessings on his creatures. We can't say when this first gift began to be, but we do know that wonderful things have taken place there within the passage of created time.

Having been born into a Christian family, I had known from my earliest days that God is the maker of heaven and earth. But that fact did not become real to me until St. Francis de Sales told me—I must

have been in my early 20s at the time—in his *Introduction to the Devout Life:*

> Consider that a certain number of years ago you were not yet in the world and that your being was a mere nothing. Where were we, O my soul, at that time...God has drawn you out of this nothing to make you what you now are.

I have not yet come fully to realize the implications of my having been drawn out of nothing by the Creator and held in existence by him. But I often consider my dependent state and God's power and love in bringing me and everyone and everything out of nothing. And especially do I ponder it at Easter, when we see that power and love acting in a new and previously unheard of way in the Resurrection. God's ingenuity was not exhausted in that first material creation. There is more to come. More has come! In Christ the First Fruits there is the new, improved humanity, the continuation of creation, the ultimate result (so far as we are concerned, I suppose) of the big bang. We can't put a date on the first appearance of matter out of nothing, but we can put a date on the beginning of matter's glorious transformation in our resurrected Lord.

And we can't place a date at the other end of time, at least not yet. It will indeed be on a date within our earthly scheme of time when our Lord Jesus Christ comes in glory to finish this present phase of creation's being and to perfect the new one. So with the Abbey Letter dating, we name the two great events of Christmas and Easter, which have anniversaries to celebrate on dates that at least reflect historical reality. And with them we use vague temporal names of the seasons of the year to remember two equally stupendous undatable realities that ought to have a place somewhere in our brain and our heart at every moment of every day, even if they have no special place in the Church's liturgical year.

Part One:

CHRISTMAS

Three to Get Ready
By Fr. William

From the Christmas 2003 Abbey Letter

"You won't believe what I'm looking at!" the woman in the department store exclaimed into her cell phone. I couldn't help overhearing her conversation. I was shopping for the monastery, and she was blocking my aisle. It's barely September, and there's a Christmas display. There are reindeer and elves and trees with little lights! ... I know! Did you ever hear of such a thing?

You can see the logic of the stores' starting Christmas early. (Although I agree with my fellow shopper, a couple of days after August is carrying things too far. Way too far.) The stores sell the things people use for their Christmas celebrations: the presents, wrappings, cards, decorations, and holiday foods. To be able to use these things on Christmas, people have to obtain them ahead of time. And decorating the stores to go with the holiday merchandise makes sense, too. It sets an appropriate mood, and reminds people not to put off holiday preparations until the last minute.

The Church offers a similar reminder in Advent, the three or four weeks before Christmas. The holiday preparations she reminds us of can be summed up in the words of Joel 4:12, which I used to see on homemade signs by country roads in the North Carolina of my childhood, "Prepare to meet thy God!"

11

We church people use Advent to prepare to meet the Lord in our celebration of his birth on Christmas, and also to prepare ourselves for the meetings with God we look forward to at the end of our earthly lives and the end of the world. We prepare by purifying ourselves, by listening to what God has to say to us and trying to understand it, and by nurturing our desire to be with our Lord. And like the holiday preparations offered by the stores, these preparations should not be put off until the last minute.

Perhaps purifying ourselves is too highfalutin an expression. What we need to do is get cleaned up and ready for our meeting with Jesus. Of course we meet the Lord in all sorts of ways, sometimes very much by surprise. And part of what's good about that is that these meetings are a normal part of our everyday life in Christ and don't call for special preparations. They're like the meetings we have when we pass a co-worker in the hall, or come across a close friend in the grocery store. But the more solemn meetings for which Advent prepares us are more like a very important date, or perhaps a special anniversary dinner. We want to get cleaned up and to look our best, to honor the occasion and the one we're meeting with. The way we clean and dress up our souls is by examining our consciences, confessing our sins, resolving to live better lives, and by doing good where, before, we had done what was not good.

Advent is also the time to take particular care to listen to the word of God. Remember, we're talking about listening as preparation for meeting our God. So we come to the Bible to hear what God has to say about what sort of people we ought to be, and what our relationships with each other and with God ought to be like. And we work to avoid our usual ways of not listening. One thing we need to avoid is thinking of other things while our beloved speaks to us. And we mustn't assume that since God is someone we love, someone we've listened to before, we already know what's coming and don't have to listen the way we would if we thought God might have something new to say to us. Both of these failures in listening can happen in long-standing relationships, even the Christian's relationship with Christ. But part of our preparation is to take special care to keep them from happening as we listen to God's word at this time.

The third part of our preparation, nurturing our desire to be with our Lord, is delicate and tricky. We can't force ourselves to be excited about the Lord's coming, or force ourselves to be eager to celebrate that coming. But, just as we can deliberately pay attention while we're listening to God, so we can pay attention to the aspects of drawing near to God that really do appeal to us. And we give thanks for those moments, and look forward to them and nurture them. The secular celebration of Christmas can be a support to us in this area. After all, it isn't entirely secular, really. And I don't usually call it secular. I tend to call it shopping Christmas. It's not all shops and shopping, either. But the name seems to work because of the newspapers' notice, X more shopping days until Christmas.

Shopping Christmas does have its red-nosed reindeer and singing chipmunks, but it also offers us bits of the gospel story, and much sacred music, live and recorded. Presents and cards we send and receive and checks made out to our favorite charities speak to us of love and giving. And so do the multitudes. Look at a busy sidewalk or crowded store and remember that it was love for each one of those people that moved the Word to become flesh and dwell among us. We can use thoughts like these to fuel our eagerness to meet the Lord at Church Christmas.

That's my name for the Christmas that begins on December 25th, the day shopping Christmas ends. Some Christians don't bother with trying to juggle the two Christmases. They integrate them and rejoice in the Messiah's nativity in a season (briefer than the shopping days before Christmas) that reaches its grand finale on Christmas day. But we Anglicans treat Christmas as the astounding opening scene of the season of the church year set aside to ponder the great meeting in which God became one of us for love of us. That's why we make the weeks before that day one of the seasons when we obey the prophet's, and God's, command to prepare ourselves to meet our God.

Welcoming Jesus
By Abbot Andrew

From the Christmas 2005 Abbey Letter

Jesus' birthday is celebrated with such abandon in many parts of the world that one might think that Jesus is the most popular person who ever lived. Jesus is so popular that we all want to welcome him with open arms, at least once a year. Or do we? A look at what the Gospels tell about the birth of Jesus tells us that welcoming his birth is no easy task.

Mary was much perplexed before accepting Gabriel's request that she invite Jesus into her womb. When Joseph realized that his betrothed, Mary, had conceived a child that could not be his, his first reaction was to send Mary and the unborn child away. It was up to Gabriel to change his mind about that. When Jesus was born in Joseph's ancestral city of Bethlehem because of the registration required by the emperor Augustus, there was no room for him anywhere in the city. Only when their fear of the Glory of the Lord was calmed did the shepherds hasten to Bethlehem to see the new-born child. The emperor welcomed the child by accepting the tally scroll his agents created for him. Three magi from the East came to Judea to pay homage to the child, but King Herod had no room for Jesus anywhere. He sent his agents to erase the child from the census figures altogether, only to be foiled by the magi and Joseph. John tells us that the Word who was with God and was God from the beginning became flesh and lived among us. But the world did not know him and did not accept him. If Jesus is subject to such a worldwide rejection, can we be so sure that we do not reject him as well?

To the Emperor Augustus, Jesus was just one more cipher on a scroll, but King Herod was smart enough to realize that this child threatened to usurp his throne. We may think that we aren't like the Emperor Augustus or King Herod because we are not rulers, but we had better think again. If we want to rule our own lives, then Jesus poses the same threat to each of us that he poses to Augustus and Herod. If we let Jesus live, Jesus will take over our lives and rule our hearts. If we want to rule our own lives, we had better reduce this child to a statistic or get rid of him altogether. We had better kill anything in our hearts that would make room for this child, or our hearts will melt with God's love for the world that was so great that he gave us his only begotten son. Herod chose to attempt to destroy the Christ Child. Joseph, his own world turned upside down by Jesus' birth, chose to welcome him and protect him. Today, Jesus presents the same choice to us: Will we welcome him into our hearts and let him rule our lives?

Origins
by Br. Martin

From the Christmas 2000 Abbey Letter

In the spring of 1999 I spent about a week visiting my dad and stepmom and my two brothers and their families. This was the first time we had all been together at the same place at the same time since 1978. Then in the autumn of that year my mom and oldest brother Danny and his wife Becky came to visit me at the Abbey. This was the first time we were able to be together since 1980. (However, I had visited all of them a number of times separately over the years.)

These visits were interesting in that they afforded me an opportunity to observe the dynamics of our relationships with each other and to see the physical similarities and differences among us. My twin brother Kevin is taller than I am, taking after our Dad. I, on the other had, am the little one of the family, a trait which comes from Mom, but I have thick blond hair and blue eyes, which I get from Dad. In facial features I resemble Dad, while Kevin is closer in

appearance to Mom. Our older brother Danny is a physically more balanced combination of physical features of our parents.

Kevin and I can generally be characterized as opposite of each other. As kids, he was outgoing while I was more reserved. He built model planes, I built model cars. He liked the early Beatles, I preferred the late Beatles. He got married, and I remained single. Politically he is conservative, I am a staunch liberal. Yet during my visit with him I became aware of the similarities that are the foundation of these differences. We both built models, we both liked the Beatles, and we both can be passionate about our politics. Again, Danny occupies a middle ground between our extremes.

In thinking about such things, I began to reflect on how it took two specific individuals, our parents, to produce the particular individuals that we are. If either of our parents had been a different person, my brothers and I would never have existed. Realizing this was something of a shock for me, for I had always assumed unthinkingly that I would still have been born, but would have been merely a bit different from what I am now. But, in fact, I wouldn't have been born at all. And this applies to everybody, both those who came before us and those who will come after.

As Christmas approaches, such thoughts lead me to ponder the family origins of Jesus. I used to think that the genealogies in the gospels of Matthew and Luke as two of the most boring passages in the New Testament. But they became interesting for me once I began to pay attention and realize what a less than ideal group of people are listed as Jesus' ancestors. Like all of us, Jesus' family had its share of family secrets. There were fathers willing to sacrifice their sons, brothers who cheated their brothers, slave owners, adulterers, polygamists, tyrants, murderers, and gentiles! Yet it is this particular group of people that literally made the Blessed Virgin Mary possible, and through her, Jesus. If even only one of these individuals had been different, the Jesus we know would never have existed.

As I ruminate along these lines, I cannot help but become a little more aware of how like us Jesus is in his humanity, and also how unique he is in his individuality. It makes me a bit more aware of how precious and special he is. It also makes me more aware of how precious and special all of us are. And it reminds me of St. Paul's teaching that we are all members one of another and of the body of Christ, in our unique individualities.

Good Enough for God
By Br. Abraham

From the Christmas 2004 Abbey Letter

Christmas lasts a long time in the monastery, as it does in the rest of America. We do it backwards from most people, though. Instead of starting the Christmas season immediately after Thanksgiving Day and then moving on to other things shortly after the 25th of December, we wait until late Christmas Eve to begin the celebration. We continue through twelve official days of Christmas and then let it slowly fade until February 2nd, when we remember the presentation of the infant Jesus in the temple. Included in the celebrations are the remembrances on January 1st of the naming and circumcision of Jesus (the Feast of the Holy Name) eight days after the celebration of his birth, and on January 6th of the visit of the wise men from the east (the Feast of the Epiphany).

The holiday on January 1st is one of my favorites in the Christmas season, because it reminds me that all of human life is important to God, not just the things that we tend to think of as spiritual. It reminds me that human life is important to God, individual humans are important to God, and human activities are important to God. In fact, all of those things are so important that God freely became a human and participated in all the common activities associated with that particular human Jesus of Nazareth. On the first day of every new year, at this Feast of the Holy Name, we celebrate two of those common human activities: the naming of a child, and the circumcision of a child.

The naming of a child is an important decision for the parents. Several lists of names are usually considered before they eventually decide on one or two or three to give the child. The Bible tells us that Mary and Joseph were spared all the work of choosing a name for their son, because an angel had already said that the name was to be Jesus. Where I grew up in Texas, Jesus was a common name, although most of my classmates with that name usually used a nickname like Chuy or Beto or Junior. It was only on the first day of school when the class roll was called that we ever heard their real name (usually mispronounced by the Anglo teacher as Geezus instead of Haysoos). The name Jesus is not uncommon up here in the Midwest either, although most of the time it is anglicized into Joshua, as it is in the Old Testament of ordinary English Bibles. Neither was the name uncommon in Jesus'

time. In fact, the prisoner who was released by Pilate instead of Jesus was named Jesus Barabbas. A common human name was good enough for God.

The circumcision of a son is also an important decision for parents. Once again, Mary and Joseph were spared that decision because in their time and place, it was simply the thing to do. It was a common, although quite meaningful, human activity and it was good enough for God.

The circumcision of Jesus also reminds us that Jesus had all his human body parts. A common human body was good enough for God. In the Gospel according to Luke, we hear a little about Jesus' childhood and adolescence. Not many details are given, but twice in the book we are told that Jesus grew just as any boy is expected to do. A common human childhood and adolescence seem to have been good enough for God, too, and even though his later years were a little extraordinary, they were lived out in the ordinary society of the time and place. In fact, if we believe it when we say that Jesus is fully God and fully human, we are saying that we believe every human bodily function, every human urge and desire, and every human fear, joy, pleasure, and pain were experienced by God in Jesus. All of those things belonged to Jesus, and therefore they belong to God. Since whatever belongs to God is holy, then all of human life is holy: every bodily function, every urge and desire, and every fear, joy, pleasure, and pain. Because of creation, we bear God's image, and because of the Incarnation, God bears our image. We are doubly holy.

That makes us doubly responsible for treating ourselves and each other as the holy beings that we are. We must take care of our holy human bodies, as well as our holy human spirits and souls. Our bodies, minds, and emotions need proper care to function as best they can. Our intellectual, sexual, social, and family lives must never be abused or neglected. Mistreatment or improper use of any parts of our lives mocks their holiness and degrades the entire human race. We don't always seem very holy to ourselves or to others, but that is because we are human, and humans grow. We must foster and cultivate our growth in holiness just as we must foster our physical and mental growth.

As our holiness grows, we see the holiness of others more clearly.

We begin to realize that our immature ideas of holiness might have been wrong, and we realize that even though others are different from us, they are holy nonetheless. However, even before we reach total maturity we are obliged to treat every person as the doubly holy image of God whether or not we can see their holiness, and whether or not they are growing in that image, or are stagnant, or are even actively trying to erase the image of God from their lives. That obligation is not an easy task. It is hard work, and we fail at it a lot of the time. We all need to work at it, every day and every hour. We can grow only with God's help, but we still need to put that help to work through prayer, honest self examination, and other disciplines. Fortunately, we have an example of growth and holiness set before us in the particular, common human life of Jesus of Nazareth. As noted preacher Barbara Brown Taylor once said: "He did not come to put us to shame with his divinity. He came to call us into the fullness of our humanity, which was good enough for him."

Where Your Heart Is
By Fr. William

Christmas 1999 Abbey Letter

Since the secular celebration of Christmas starts around Thanksgiving time, it is perhaps understandable that I grew up uncertain whether Over the River and Through the Woods was a Thanksgiving song or a Christmas song. (One of our monks, who taught music in the grades in which I sang that rollicking number, assures me it is the latter.) My confusion was aggravated by the fact that both holidays hold some imagery in common: turkeys, for instance, and the subject of this very song, a visit to snowy-haired grandparents on a snow-covered farm.

In my North Carolina childhood, I had grandparents who lived on a farm. My grandmother's hair was white, too-magnificently white. My folks would cut our Christmas tree at the farm, always a red cedar. We also might gather some holly branches, and mistletoe. This last was the exciting part. We didn't climb a tree and cut the mistletoe. We were Presbyterians, not Druids. The men shot it down with a rifle. But visits to my mother's parents weren't restricted to the

holidays. Their home was just a few hours drive away, close enough for us to visit frequently. When the time came for one of these visits, my mother would tell us to get in the car, we were going home. We kids played and fought in the back seat. We counted cows and read Burma Shave signs. And the whole family sang. Long songs, mostly: "Down by the River Side," for example, and "When the Saints Go Marching In." When we sang that last one, we included the stanzas about the stars beginning to fall, the sun refusing to shine, and the moon turning into blood. That was fun because I never got to sing those bits at school or at camp. There were secular songs, too. It was years before I realized that when my father sang "Hinky dinky parlezvous," it wasn't because he had forgotten the words for that part of "Mademoiselle from Armentières," but because those were the words.

When we arrived, there were our beloved grandparents to visit, as well as other relatives in the area. And we would play, either by ourselves or with cousins. My grandmother had a gallon jar of old buttons we would sort. And there were shelves of books from an earlier time. I recall the stamp album with page after of page of countries that no longer existed in my childhood, countries that have reappeared in the last decade. Outside, we were constantly building forts and camps, and defending the barns from invisible invaders. Or we boys would cut cane spears and throw them into wasp's nests the size of dinner plates. The wasps had their own way of dealing with invaders. There were also

things that involved the oversight of an adult. We might go fishing or swimming in the pond. Or we might hunt for stone arrowheads in a freshly plowed field. We might pick beans, a thing I hated to do, and string them, which I hated even more. Or sometimes we would gather eggs, a thing which I loved to do. Hens would lay eggs in the most peculiar places. They were especially fond of the soft dirt under the porches. But, whatever we did on a given visit, our time on the farm, our time with our extended family, would run out. My folks would load up the luggage and tell us it was time to go home.

That announcement had me stumped. If my mother called going from our house in Gastonia to the farm in Eagle Springs going home, how could traveling in the opposite direction also be called going home? This was one of the great linguistic mysteries of my childhood. I understand it well enough now, of course. Because when I leave the Abbey to visit my folks in the house where I grew up, I'm going home. And when my time there is over, and I get on the airplane for Michigan, that's going home too. So, those are my homes.

But where is God's home? A quick answer is heaven. But quick answers aren't always reliable when we're talking about the one who is omnipresent and eternal. In reality, God doesn't have a home any more than he has a bedroom. All the definitions I've seen of home make it out to be a place that is somehow the proper place for a given person, as distinct from all other places. But there is no place where God doesn't belong. I think God's home (since I am speaking so) must be God himself. The holy Trinity dwells in perfect and changeless unity and simplicity. God dwells "in light inaccessible from before time and for ever."

When the baby Jesus was born in Bethlehem, God, the eternal Word, gained a second home. The earth was now his home, the children of Adam were now his blood kin. There was a particular place where he grew up. He played there and learned there. He knew the sounds and smells of that house, of that village. He knew which words Joseph sang to which tunes. Of course, the eternal Logos knew those things eternally. But when the baby Jesus grew up, he remembered them.

Or should say that when Christ was born, he began to have many homes? As a man, he lived all the ambiguities and complexities around that word that so confused me as a child. Certainly, Nazareth was his childhood home, as Gastonia was mine, and Eagle Springs my mother's. But he left Nazareth. Did he think of Capernaum as home? Or did he think of home as a place he had left, without ever finding another home as an addition or a replacement?

That's the sort of thing we'll have to wait to find out. But our faith has given us a few answers about Jesus' homes already. Because we call him the Messiah, we must call Israel his home. And because we call him the fully human son of Mary, we must call this earth his home, too. And because earth has become his home, Jesus, like so many of us, can be going home on each leg of a round trip. He went home when he ascended into heaven. But when he returns in glory (and the sun refuses to shine, and the stars begin to fall, and the moon turns into blood), he will be coming home then, too.

But he won't be coming home to a very nice place, I'm afraid. This world is a place of sin and suffering and death. And that is actually why he made it his home. He was born among us, as one of us, to save us from just these things. In order to save us, the one who assumed our flesh has called us to be members of his body. And when we do that, we make a Ruth and Naomi sort of commitment: "Intreat me not to leave thee, or to return from following after thee: for whither thou goest, I will go; and where thou lodgest, I will lodge: thy people shall be my people, and thy God my God." In other words, Jesus' homes are our homes, his everlasting home is our everlasting home. And when the saints go marching in, they will be going home. That's odd in a way. Heaven is a place we've never been. And how can a place we've never been be our home?

Look at the manger scene you've arranged for Christmas. See where the baby is now. This isn't home. Home is Nazareth. The manger is in Bethlehem. And after Bethlehem comes exile in Egypt. Nazareth is a long way from Egypt—over the river Nile, and through the woods of Galilee. When the Lord Jesus finally enters his earthly home (walking in, it wouldn't surprise me, on his own two feet), he is coming home to a place he's never been before.

In his new home, the child will have new places to explore, new things to learn. And he will know his parents' love in a new setting, where it will be expressed in new ways. When the glorified Jesus leads his adopted family into their new home, they'll have those things, too. I want to be in that number. I want to see him in the flesh he assumed for our sake. And I want to see beyond that flesh, to see the glory of the God who made this world and that one.

Jesus wants me to see that glory as well. He wants us all to see his glory in our new home. On the eve of his death he prayed, "Father, I desire that those also, whom you have given me, may be with me where I am, to see my glory, which you have given me because you loved me before the foundation of the world."

Joy to the World?

By Br. Cuthbert

From the Christmas 2007 Abbey Letter

Christmas is nearly upon us again, and for many, the yearly remembrance of our Lord's birth brings with it a sense of renewal and hope for the future. In most parts of the northern hemisphere, the earth lies dormant; not barren and lifeless but rather in a purifying slumber that tells us it will once again burst forth in life. The liturgical year began anew on December 2nd and hopefully for all of us the season of Advent has afforded us the chance to reflect on the past year while looking forward to the new one.

But something just doesn't feel right. Our leaders speak of a never-ending war as we say, Peace on earth, goodwill towards men. We decry the commercialism of Christmas but then turn and lament when cashiers won't say, "Merry Christmas." While many may dream of chestnuts roasting on an open fire, still there are many who are faced with the reality of being unable to afford

28

heating costs, or health care, or a decent meal. Something is not right. It has been said, many times many ways, that it is easy to get so caught up in the details of preparing for Christmas that we can lose sight of what Christmas is about. Christmas is about the Gospel. But quite apart from the normal distractions of the holiday season, if any of the above contradictions ring true—and I believe they do—then a fair question to ask is, What *is* the Gospel?

Certainly we know the story. There's a hay-filled manger with all kinds of animals nearby. There's the Virgin Mary and the baby Jesus and St. Joseph. There's the star and three wise men bringing gold, frankincense, and myrrh. There's an angel and some shepherds. It all makes for a pretty scene adorning a mantle piece—or for those who really splash out, a front yard—and it does remind us of the narrative. I do not wish to discount the value of knowing the Nativity story, but the question still remains: What is the good news? What is the meaning behind the Christmas story that makes having all those trinkets worthwhile?

If here you are hoping for a simple Jesus saves kind of answer, dear reader, I am afraid you will be disappointed. The fact is that in merely having to ask, What is the Gospel? an even more unsettling question arises: *Is* there a Gospel? Is there any good news at all? In a world that is dominated by rampant materialism, a notion that all things can be explained by quantitative formulae, and a relativism that denies even the possibility of abiding truth, there is precious little room for a newborn baby who, some claim, is the savior of the world.

It is no wonder so many people detest the Christmas season. All this talk of peace, love, hope, and joy does not mesh with the prevailing worldview that measures peace in terms of how much or how little violence is going on, that equates hope with a decent retirement package, and that discounts love and joy as nothing more than chemical reactions that can be manipulated. If all this leaves one thinking that life has no meaning, it is not hard to see why. The mentality of pointlessness, however, does not seem to lead always to despair. Instead, the coping mechanism of cynicism steps in, allowing many people to laugh at the perceived absurdity of the world: There is no need for good news because nothing is wrong and nothing is right. It is what it is and there is nothing meaningful to say. So much for the Gospel, right?

The problem with this postmodern worldview, though, is that it can paralyze the human spirit. The cynical answer here is, There is no such thing as the human spirit, but that just makes the paralysis easier to ignore. The point is clear enough: if there is nothing to the notion of a shared humanity, then the ideas of justice, responsibility, equality, and human rights have no claim on us. Indeed, if we flat out reject the concept of a human nature that is more than just biological similarity, then the result is a complete isolation of the individual in which actions only have meaning for the person who performs them, and any impact on other people's lives cannot be viewed objectively as either good or bad. Some see this as true freedom. Others, including myself, see it as the epitome of slavery.

Another way of coping with a worldview devoid of meaning is to adopt a rigid fundamentalism. This involves a firm declaration of belief that there is real meaning in life, but it also requires the total rejection of any fact or idea, however valid, that does not fit with one's picture of reality. At first, such a stance may be comforting to those seeking something concrete on which to pin their hopes, but it invariably leads to a mentality of exclusion that is just as poisonous to the human spirit as any postmodern way of thinking—and perhaps even more so. If, runs the fundamentalist mind-set, you do not believe exactly what I believe and act exactly as I say you should, you do not deserve my respect. Subconsciously or not, this attitude can lead to a gradation of humanity; those of the in crowd being human, and everyone else somewhat less so. Grading humanity in this way makes it easier to label others as enemies who either need to change completely or be eliminated. In a system like this, the only good news is belonging to the in crowd. It's bad news for everyone else.

These two ways of dealing with life's contradictions—shrugging one's shoulders and saying, It's all meaningless anyway, or claiming that everything will be ok when our enemies are converted or destroyed— are equally unsatisfying because both views degrade the relationship that human beings have to one another and their surroundings. To the fundamentalist, it's a hard-line us and them, so life's contradictions are

not seen as contradictions because somebody has to be the bad guy. To the postmodernist, it's neither us nor them but an unconnected collection of me's, and there need not be any sense of contradiction at all because there is no objective standard according to which actions have meaning.

It's hard to reconcile the meaning of Christmas with such worldviews. That is because the message behind the story is about relationship: God embraces humanity. The love that created and holds all things in being—not an impersonal force or abstract concept of philosophical speculation, but the living energy that gives life to the world—stepped fully into the human condition. There, in that manger, was placed the ultimate expression of humanity's relationship to existence. In the manger is God's message that humanity does not consist of us and them but rather is one; only us. For all the strife and separation, for all the alienation and conflict there is in the world, in the manger is God's message that humanity does not stand abandoned and isolated. God is with us. The pervasive yet unmoving love that sustains existence makes its home in our humanity. Joy to the world? Emphatically yes!

But still something does not seem right. Life's contradictions persist. God may be incarnate, but the world still seems as crazy as ever. Here it is good to remember that it was into such a world that our Lord was born and that he spent much of his public ministry exposing hypocrisy and contradictions and caring for those who, according to the prevailing worldview of the time, were seen as less than human. If anything should strike us about Jesus, it should be his uncompromising humanity.

And, my friends, we are called to follow his example. We are called to be radically honest about the world's contradictions (our own as well as those of others), to recognize where incongruities can lead to dehumanization, and to cry foul whenever and wherever we see the forces of dehumanization at work. Also, in the face of such contradictions, we are called to care for those who have been made outcasts and to persist in proclaiming a message of joy, peace, and hope; of a joy that is founded on God's intimate involvement in humanity, of a peace that is based on a true understanding of our shared humanity, and of a hope for the future of that humanity so glorious that it can truly be described as not of this world. Undoubtedly, taking such a stand is not easy, and in many cases, doing so will meet with derision. Jesus warned us that this would be the case. But if it means restoring a sense of worth and belonging even to one person out of a hundred, the stand is worth taking.

Rejoice ... The Lord is with You!
By Br. Martin

From the Christmas 2002 Abbey Letter

One of the themes I have come to appreciate most in the Christmas story is that of God's being among us, of becoming one of us not in majesty and power but sharing in our humanity in all the struggles and trials that implies. I derive much hope and peace from the fact that God meets us where we are, dwelling within the circumstances of our lives, using each situation to bring us closer and closer to his most loving heart.

God is with us. Our lives are drenched with God's presence and involvement, even though we may not be able to see it in any given situation, except perhaps in hindsight. And it's okay if we cannot see how God is working in our lives. We are, after all, too close to see the big picture. This is where faith comes to our aid; some things have to be believed to be seen.

We are all on a journey, and we are all in this together. And while the destination is not unimportant (to understate it), we must understand that it is the journey itself that prepares us for the destination. This is why Jesus keeps calling us to love one another, for we can only make the journey supporting each other.

Our destination is of course union with God, a concept so wonderful in light of the Incarnation that our minds can just barely begin to comprehend what that means. Even though our destination is God, let us not forget that God is with us, using the journey of our lives and the means through which our goal will be achieved. And during those inevitable and unavoidable dark periods, let us remember Gabriel's words to Mary, Rejoice, so highly favored! The Lord is with you!

A Hide and Seek Prayer
By Fr. William

From the Christmas 2010 Abbey Letter

The Second Sunday after Christmas is one of those funny Sundays that starts a week that ends up being taken over by some other liturgical observance. In this case, on the sixth of January the Epiphany collect is used and continues to be used for the rest of that week, and the collect for the Second Sunday after Christmas retires until next year. (Accented on the first syllable, a collect is the principal brief prayer summing up the theme of the day or of a liturgical action.)

Actually, that prayer doesn't always stay retired for a whole year. It can pop up again here or there. If your church reads the Creation story as a lesson in the Easter Vigil, you will find the collect following that lesson is our friend, the collect for the Second Sunday after Christmas:

O God, who wonderfully created, and yet more wonderfully restored, the dignity of human nature: Grant that we may share the divine life of him who humbled himself to share our humanity, your Son Jesus Christ; who lives and reigns with you, in the unity of the Holy Spirit, one God, for ever and ever. Amen.

The prayer itself is old. Our first written copy of it is in the Leonine Sacramentary, a seventh-century collection of prayers offered by the celebrant at various liturgies, where it is the collect for the first Mass of Christmas Day. But in spite of its beauty and antiquity, it only appeared in the Book of Common Prayer in the current 1979 edition.

That doesn't mean that it didn't sneak into our churches earlier than its official admission, though. Around the eleventh century, this prayer was very slightly modified and became a standard part of the offertory of the Roman Mass. While a bit of water was being added to the wine in the chalice, the priest would pray our prayer, but saying, Grant that, through the mystery of this water and wine, we may share the divine life of him.... As some Anglican priests began using the private prayers of the Latin liturgy in Anglican services, this became the standard prayer said while water was blessed and added to the chalice in many Episcopal celebrations of the Eucharist. So folks may well have been at lots of services where the prayer was used, but it was used so quietly they didn't know. And for those of us who did know the prayer over the water, finding it as a Christmas collect was like coming across an old friend in her new job. You smile real big and say, When did you start working here?

Adding water to the wine at the offertory, the mixed chalice as it is called, was quite shocking and controversial when Anglo-Catholic priests labored to bring it back in the nineteenth century, but through the years it has become the standard practice among high church and low alike. The two cruets on the credence shelf were one of the things that impressed me when I first saw a chapel set up for the Holy Communion back when I was a Presbyterian kid at the Episcopal diocesan church camp in Western North Carolina. I confess I did completely misread the setup. I thought those worldly, sophisticated, Episcopal communicants were being offered their choice of red or white wine. That would have been hospitable, perhaps. But it wouldn't have been as good as water and wine.

No, there are good reasons the mixed chalice won out over a cup of plain wine, or my imagined choice of wines. In the first place, it was the custom of people in our Lord's time and place to add water to the wine they drank. So we suppose Jesus himself did that, and doing what Jesus

did can be a way for us to draw closer to him. Also, because wine and blood are so closely linked in the Christian imagination, the mixture also recalls the water and blood that flowed from Christ's heart at the crucifixion. And historically there have been many offertory prayers that emphasize that facet of the mystery of this water and wine. But I think the richest meaning, or meanings, are the ones spoken of in the collect we're considering now.

God wonderfully created, and yet more wonderfully restored, the dignity of human nature. The mixed chalice recalls this. As we read in that first lesson in the Easter Vigil, there was water in the beginning, when the Spirit of God brooded over the deep. When we were formed from the dust of the earth, a lot of water must have gone into the mix, since our bodies are a bit over half water to this day. But we made a lot of bad choices and didn't treat our nature as the dignified thing it was, so God had to fix a creation gone wrong to restore that dignity. And that was accomplished by the blood of Christ, shed on the cross for our salvation. The water and wine in the cup very naturally proclaim the dual mystery of our creation and redemption. Jesus' blood is the drink of restored humanity. We who failed to live up to the challenge of drinking the plain water of our creation today find ourselves drinking the rich, heavenly wine of our eternal salvation. Water shows where we've come from. Wine shows where we are going.

The one who shed that blood, who died on the cross, and rose again, was not simply God the Son, the eternal Logos, appearing among us as a divine apparition. The deathless one humbled himself to share our humanity. The divine person assumed our human nature. That's the first of the two Christmas presents the prayer speaks of, the Word made flesh. The Son is the Father's gift to us. But the Father isn't the only one giving us this gift surpassing all others. The Lord became incarnate by the Holy Ghost and the Virgin Mary. So the baby Jesus is a gift to us from them as well.

He is a Christmas gift to the entire human race. But not only does he share our human life, he came to redeem it, and share his eternal divine life with his brothers and sisters. That's the second Christmas present from above. Just as the Father gave us the Son to be born as one of us, so the Son gives us the Father, reconciling sinners to their perfectly righteous Creator. And again, that's a gift the very giving of which has been shared. Not only is our share in divine life a gift from Jesus himself, it's a gift from everyone who has ever brought us closer to Jesus. And the same Holy Spirit who worked through others to bring us that gift can work through us to share it with others, bringing them closer to Jesus, who himself brings them into the life of the Holy Trinity.

That can be another meaning of the mystery of water and wine. We add the water of our witness and testimony to the wine of Christ's saving work. What we have to offer is nothing compared to what he has accomplished. But he accepts and commissions us to share the saving work of restoring our sisters and brothers to the glorious dignity meant for us from the beginning, and won for us on Calvary.

Making Peace
By Abbot Andrew

From the Christmas 2006 Abbey Letter

Glory to God in the highest heaven, and on earth peace among those whom he favors. Lk. 2:14

The shepherds kneeling in adoration before a newborn child sleeping in a manger is an image of peace. The three Magi from the East kneeling down in homage and giving valuable gifts to the newborn child is another image of peace. Together, these two images illustrate the angels' song: Glory to God in the highest heaven, and on earth peace among those whom he favors. The richest and the lowest classes of humanity unite in worship of the Christ Child, the Messiah, the Prince of Peace.

That's the Good News. The bad news is that other images and events in the narratives of Jesus' birth undermine these images of peace. John says that the Word that became flesh came to what was his own, and his own people did not accept him. Luke fleshes out John's words by telling us that Jesus was laid in a manger because there was no place for them in the inn. Although most nativity scenes locate the manger in a stable, there is nothing in the text that says the manger was sheltered at all. The Holy Family may well have been left out in the cold. The group of shepherds, who were sent by the angels to the manger where Jesus lay, may remind us of King David, who was a shepherd in his youth. In Jesus' time, however, shepherds were very close to the bottom of the social scale in the eyes of both Jews and Romans. That is, Jesus, himself an outcast at birth, was adored by fellow outcasts.

The journey to Bethlehem was a result of an imperial decree by the Emperor Augustus that all people should be registered and accounted for. This attempt to put everybody in their place was one aspect of the widely celebrated *Pax Romana*, the Roman Peace. Ironically, this peaceful ordering of the Empire required Joseph to go to his own town with his pregnant wife where, it turned out, there was no room for them. More troubling, King Herod, a client king in the Roman Empire, shows us just how violent life could be under the Roman peace. When the Magi asked Herod where the king of the Jews had been born, Herod was frightened, and all Jerusalem with him. When Herod realized that the Magi had avoided him on their return journey, he ordered the murder of all boys in Bethlehem under the age of two. Some thirty years later, Jesus would find out for himself how peaceful the Roman peace was for somebody like him. The angels' song, then, is not only a religious statement; it is a political statement. It is not the Roman emperor but Christ who truly establishes peace.

In highlighting Jesus' vulnerability in these ways, the story of Jesus' birth challenges us to examine our attitude to our own vulnerability and the vulnerability of others. In contrast with the Word made flesh, we usually do not wish to be vulnerable in any way, and we do everything possible to avoid it. In the process of trying to make ourselves invulnerable, we usually end up preying on the vulnerability of other people. It is, then, all the more amazing that the one Being in the universe who really is invulnerable chooses to be vulnerable, even to extent of being born in harsh circumstances and dying under circumstances harsher still. If we despise vulnerability in ourselves, do we then despise vulnerability in others? Even, or especially, if it is God who is vulnerable? Do we choose to welcome and protect the vulnerable Christ Child as did Mary, Joseph, the shepherds and the Magi? Does the image of a newborn babe lying in a feeding trough make us wish to do something about it? That is the sentiment in a lullaby carol I sang as a chorister: "I will give you a coat of fur."

Welcoming and caring for a vulnerable person increases our own vulnerability, as Herod knew very well. Being vulnerable means that we risk being hurt, perhaps hurt very badly. What could possess any of us to choose to be so vulnerable? What could ever possess God to make such a choice? The only answer I can think of is Love. In our own human experience, love is the only thing that motivates us to choose to be vulnerable to another to the extent of serving that other. Caring for a helpless baby makes us vulnerable to the way the helpless child will react to the love and protection we give. There can be no clearer proof that God is love than the birth of the Christ Child in Bethlehem. Later in life, Jesus said that he came not to be served but to serve. Knowing how vulnerable his serving us would make him, he added that he had come to give his life a ransom for many. But in his very vulnerability, especially as a newborn child, Jesus himself needed to be served by us. In the Lauds hymn during the Christmas season, we sing that "the blest creator of the earth ...through whom the very birds are fed" depended on his earthly mother to feed him. Like any other human child, Jesus could only enter the world by human permission. One of the most probing questions inspired by the Gospels is: What if Mary had said No when Gabriel asked her to allow a child to be conceived in her womb by the Holy Spirit? Fortunately, she said instead: Let it be with me according to your word. Similarly, we can ask: What if Joseph had refused to accept the child and instead withdrew his protection of Mary and the child?

The images of peace presented in the Nativity stories affirm the vulnerability both of others and ourselves. On the other hand, all of the images of violence point to a rejection of vulnerability. The fact that vulnerability challenges us to do something makes it clear that God does not just drop peace into our laps. Peace happens when somebody does something to make it happen. Peace fails to happen not only when we commit acts of violence but when we do not care enough to do anything at all. In the Beatitudes, Jesus did not say: Blessed are those who don't mind if there happens to be peace. Jesus said: Blessed are the peacemakers. Peace is something we have to make.

The story of Jesus' birth also tells us that peace originates in a willingness to mirror God's love by being vulnerable enough to welcome and nurture the Christ Child through welcoming the least of God's people. We can easily imagine the innkeeper saying, after finding out whom he had turned away, that he would have found room for the Holy Family if only he had known who they were. This very protest shows us how much Jesus identifies with all people who do not have a room on this earth. More important, lest we think we would welcome Jesus if we knew who he was, we should remember that Herod did know who the child was and he wanted to kill him. The slaughter of many children as a result of King Herod's rejection makes it clear that welcoming and protecting Jesus entails welcoming and protecting all who are vulnerable. But surely none of us would want to kill the Christ Child? Or would we? Matthew says that all Jerusalem was troubled by the news brought by the Magi. Indeed, all Jerusalem was sufficiently troubled by Jesus some thirty years later to succeed in doing what Herod tried and failed to do.

Making peace can be as simple as offering a cup of water to one of God's little ones. The importance of such simple acts as welcoming and offering water for making peace gains further emphasis when we note that Jesus counters his disciples' argument about who is the greatest by telling them to become like children. That is, they should themselves to be as vulnerable as the children. Mark shows how Jesus' own disciples continued to have a hard time getting it. Even after being told to become like children rather than fight over who is the greatest, the disciples tried to drive away the children being brought to Jesus so that he might bless them.

So maybe the simple acts that make peace aren't so simple after all. The very fact that these acts of making peace are very simple makes it easy to overlook them for the sake of arguing about who is the greatest, or playing power politics as did the Emperor Augustus. What makes these simple acts really hard is that they must be done every day, and they must be done to our neighbors, that is to the people who are right around us. Thanks to the means of communication we have now, especially the Internet, some people halfway round the world are among our neighbors. We must remain alert to opportunities for the small acts of peace that can be more important than we can guess. Christmas comes once a year, but the lessons it teaches us challenge us every day.

Part Two:

BENEDICTINE INSPIRATIONS

Monk's Best Friend
By Br. Abraham

From the Summer 2010 Abbey Letter

We are blessed with beautiful and functional architecture here at St. Gregory's, and we are grateful to our supporters around the world who have given us the funds to build a place where we can live, work, pray, and offer hospitality to guests who want to share in our life of prayer. One of my favorite parts of our monastery complex is the bell tower over the entrance to the church. Specifically, it is the bell I am so fond of. Our new bronze bell (it has been hanging in the tower about eighteen months now) is large and produces a pleasant low pitch when struck by its clapper. Our old bell is much smaller and produces a higher pitch, and was hidden in a housing on top of the old dorm until it was moved to its present housing on the roof of the current refectory/library building. Because of its housing, I have never actually seen our old bell, but the new one is hung in an open tower for all to see, and when the sun hits it at certain parts of the day, it shines brilliantly.

Both of these bells have played a big part in my life these past seventeen years that I have been at St. Gregory's, and I am grateful for what they have taught me. They have made it clear to me that as a monk, I am to possess nothing—even my time is not my own. Everything in a monastery is community property, so everything must be shared and taken care of in a way that acknowledges that someone else has a right to use the very same item. This practice of monastic poverty is not meant to express any disdain for the world or the things in the world, but rather to instill in us the utmost respect for all of God's creation. In other words, by practicing stewardship rather than possessiveness, we affirm that everything receives its integrity and legitimacy from God, not from our possession or control of it. Time is one of those things that monastic life teaches us to give up trying to control, so that we can more properly enjoy and use it as best we can to make the world a better place for ourselves and others.

The ringing of the bell marks out the schedule of the monastic day that is broken up into periods of public and private prayer, work, rest, meals, sleep, recreation, silence, private time, and group social time. It does not matter if I want to do any of those things when its time comes, or if I feel like doing them. It does not matter if I like the psalms, hymns, scriptures, or sermons at times of public prayer, or if I like the food served at mealtimes, or if I would rather be talking at silent times or alone at times of group recreation. Since time is not our own to control, monastic life mercifully takes away that illusion of possession and expects us to be where we are supposed to be when we are supposed to be there.

Following such a schedule, rather than our own desires, does not squash our personalities, as some might expect. Rather, it allows our

true selves to grow, freed from false ideas of self-importance. We slowly learn that everyone is equally and infinitely important in the eyes of God, as well as the fact that all aspects of our own personalities are important. Since every aspect of our being is important, our desire to do only the things we want to do when and how we want to do them is met with a scheduled discipline designed to help all parts grow. By allowing the monastic schedule to act as a template or structure for our lives, we can flourish in ways that we never expected. Unfortunately, we can also allow the schedule to act as a prison, stifling us and withering our personalities. Of course, it is our choice whether we willingly follow the schedule so that it can foster our growth or resist it and become irritable and sour in the struggle. Having the bell constantly calling us to leave our bed, our work or hobby, or a favorite book or website in order to gather in the church for prayer can have the effect of teaching us that all of our work, rest, and relaxation is special enough to be surrounded by prayer, or it can have the effect of driving us crazy with its demands. If we choose to answer the bell joyfully and gratefully, then more joy and gratitude will follow. If we choose to answer with bitterness at being interrupted, then only more bitterness awaits.

Choosing how we answer the call of the bell is not something we do only when we join the monastery as a postulant or move through the different stages of becoming clothed as a novice and making junior and then senior monastic professions. Every day we must decide to live the monastic life fully, and every day we know we will fail in some way. So the next morning, we must make the same determination to not let our past failures haunt us, but rather to rely on the grace of God to help us fulfill our vows.

I have also learned some other lessons from our bell. In spite of the monastic ideal of a balanced life of prayer, work, rest, and recreation, there are some days when it seems that there is too much to do—more work than there is time to finish. So I have learned the importance of managing my time well, and of admitting that I can not and should not do everything. On such days, prayer gets top priority, rest and recreation are put aside for another day, and work fills all the leftover time (and almost all pressing tasks almost always get done). At those times when work is overwhelming, it is good to think of our labor as a gift we are giving to the world, rather than as a burden that takes away our free time. We must acknowledge that the ideal of the balanced life is a goal that can not always be met while also realizing that it is not good to constantly let work consume our lives. We must learn to always do our best—no more, no less.

Another lesson I have learned is that being on time is a concrete way to show our love and respect for others, because by being on time for our appointments, we show the other persons involved that they are important to us, and that we respect their schedules. This is important in a monastery, because living in a monastery means living with other people (which is sometimes surprising to those who think that monastic life is geared solely toward the individual's relationship with God). Of course, living in a monastery does include having a relationship with God, so being on time for public prayer is a way to express our love for God, as is making time for our private prayer and scripture reading.

The bell sounds different to me throughout the day, because I am in various parts of the monastery (inside and outside) doing different things as the day progresses. I am also in different moods at different times, but by the end of the day, I am always grateful for its lessons. (At this point I must also admit that its ringing often pleasantly reminds me of two Pink Floyd albums in which certain songs make references to bells: *Dark Side of the Moon* and *The Division Bell.* However, that subject might be better addressed in another article.) I have not always been a good or willing student of our bell, but I do think it has had a positive affect on me, no matter how slight, and I do hope that I might continue under its instruction for a long time. Once again, thank you, our supporters, for making it possible to have such a bell. It rings throughout the day, bringing the monks and guests together to pray for each other and the world around us. May we joyfully heed its call.

From Discernment to Obedience
By Prior Aelred

From the Christmas 2009 Abbey Letter

In the final chapter of the *Rule* of our Holy Father Benedict, the monks are admonished to read the *Conferences* of the Fathers, their *Institutes* and their *Lives*. Although there has been some doubt expressed as to whether the *Conferences* and *Institutes* referred to are the works by those names written in the 5th century by John Cassian, current scholarly consensus is that Cassian's works are meant. The assumption is that John Cassian's condemnation at the Council of Orange (for being insufficiently Augustinian in his understanding of grace) led to St. Benedict avoiding the use of his name, while recognizing that the practical worth of his writings on the monastic life was too great to be lost. Similarly, the condemnation of Evagrius Ponticus for Origenism did not lead to the suppression of his writings, but to their continuing to circulate under the pseudonym of St. Nilus.

Whatever the accuracy of current scholarly opinion, there seems little doubt that generations of monks assumed that it was Cassian's works referred to, for, according to Owen Chadwick, it was the Benedictine monasteries that were primarily responsible for preserving the writings of Cassian.

Cassian was a monk in Palestine who traveled to Egypt to receive firsthand the stories of the early monks. Late in life, after he had settled in southern Gaul, he was asked to write something for the benefit of the monastic communities then being formed in the West and produced the *Conferences* and *Institutes.* Of course the *Conferences,* written by an old monk a quarter of a century after the time when he had first as a youth heard the stories of the Egyptian monks, cannot be considered transcripts of what was originally said. Discussions about the authenticity of speeches in historical writings are endless. Suffice it to say that Cassian's works themselves were venerated and his stories accepted as being valuable guides in the monastic pilgrimage.

The first conferences are from Abba Moses, the Ethiopian. Moses had been a brigand and killer before his conversion. Overcoming racial prejudice, he eventually came to be regarded as a wise guide in the monastic life and was even ordained to the priesthood (something extremely uncommon among the early monks).

In his second conference, Moses tells a story of Anthony the Great. Some of the elders came to see St. Anthony and spoke all night on the topic of perfection. They wanted to discover how best to attain purity of heart and union with God. Some thought that the chief means were fasting and keeping vigils. Others thought detachment the answer. Some thought solitude and seclusion the only way to avoid distractions, while they were answered by those who held that the essential virtues of hospitality and charity would be excluded by such a course. The blessed Anthony was the last to speak. His discourse in the *Conferences* is essentially an expansion of an aphorism attributed to him in the *Apothegmata Patrem:* "Some have afflicted their bodies by asceticism, but they lack discernment and are far from God."

For many people the Desert Fathers have conjured up notions of extreme and bizarre practices—contests of who could go without sleep or food for the longest period—and there are, to be sure, such stories in the collections. What one should note, however, is that the point of such stories is usually to indicate the inappropriateness of such extremities. The question of the accuracy of Cassian's account of

Moses' story about St. Anthony, or even the saying ascribed to him in the *Apothegmata,* is not essential. The fact that such an attitude was attributed to Anthony, universally revered as the first and wisest of the monks, indicates the importance the monks attached to the virtue of discernment.

When we turn to the *Rule,* we see that a major change of emphasis has occurred. First, St. Benedict prefers the related word discretion to discernment. Second, discretion is almost always to be exercised not by the individual monk, but by the Abbot (the single exception being that if one of the older monks loses his temper with one of the boys *sine discretione*). The only time Benedict uses the word discernment is in chapter II, Qualities of the Abbot: *Non ab eo persona in monasterio discernatur* (The abbot should avoid all favoritism in the monastery)— thus using the word in a meaning that approximates not our understanding of discernment, but discrimination.

It seems that the major reason for the shift in emphasis is the change from a monastic life that is basically eremitical (solitary) to one that is cenobitic (communal). Obviously the hermit, alone in his cell wrestling the demons, needed discernment in abundance, but the natural gathering of hermits into loose-knit communities around a noted elder (in the tradition of St. Anthony) and the formation of more strictly cenobitic communities in Upper Egypt (under the

leadership of St. Pachomius) led to emphasis on a different monastic virtue—obedience. If discernment is regarded as the primary virtue and the young monk discerns that he need not do what he is told, community breaks down.

Even the Abbot must be careful, it seems, and the primary monastic virtue comes to be that of doing things in accordance with the practice of the elders—meaning not just the experienced members of a monastic community, but that of earlier generations of monks. The later Desert Father stories have numerous anecdotes about how much better the monks used to be. Monks did not originate the concepts of the good old days nor we've always done it this way, but they have traditionally been among the most enthusiastic practitioners of these attitudes.

The 12th century Cistercians, with their stress on the importance of exact observance, were frequently accused of being Pharisees. Certainly this is a danger. There can be an empty formalism, devoid of any moral or religious content. On the other hand, one must remember the words of C. S. Lewis, One must be careful what one pretends to be, for what one pretends to be is what one tends to become. Monks see their life not as anything special but as the following of the Gospel, a serious attempt to live the Christian life.

As Simon Tugwell says in *Ways of Imperfection:* "... we must not forget that the monastic routine was regarded as embodying, precisely, the Christian life, and there is nothing obviously wrong in supposing that in *behaving* like Christians we gradually *become* new creatures in Christ. We rejoin here the eminently sane Augustinian principle that human minds and wills are far too erratic to provide a dependable basis for the Christian life; it is on the objective fact of the Church that we must build, leaving it to God to perfect man's inner conversion."

Terrence Kardong, author of the most recent scholarly commentary on the *Rule,* has said that one of the emphases of Cassian with which modern monks are frequently uncomfortable is the notion that the cenobite is free from care. The necessities of life are taken care of and one's time is regulated by a predictable schedule not to make the monk complacent, but to free him of the burdens of normal life so that he may concentrate on God and His will and seek inner peace and tranquility. Thus St. Bernard can argue that there is nothing to prevent the monk from tasting and seeing that the Lord is good. Monastic discipline, willingly embraced, is ultimately freeing.

According to Simon Tugwell, the monks of the West inherited an Augustinian tradition, where, "... freedom is not something we have by right from the outset, it is something which grows in us gradually as we are freed from the tyranny of the old Adam, until, in heaven, we reach the 'blessed constraint' of not being able to sin, which is perfect freedom. And the discipline of monastic observance is a radical way of denying power to our fallen instincts. The pessimistic view of monastic life as largely a way of keeping people out of mischief can be subsumed into a much more positive view of monastic life as providing space within which the new creature in Christ can come to maturity. If the cell is a tomb, it is also a womb."

Many people have been critical of outward observances as being simply going through the motions, but the unity of the monastic community comes from common observance, so that the monks are not forced to be inwardly uniform. By agreeing to an outward minimum, the monastic life allows the monks to develop inwardly in their own time and way. As the Prologue to the *Rule* states, "For as we advance in the religious life and in faith, our hearts expand and we run the way of God's commandments with unspeakable sweetness of love."

Again, Tugwell puts this very well, "The common observances provide an external point of reference, which allows monks to relax with themselves and with each other; the monastic life as a whole, undisturbed by individual quirks, becomes both a unique 'school of charity' and a continual drama of charity. The love of God and the love of neighbor are inextricably entwined in the life of inner unity of heart and outward uniformity of observance, so that the monastery can be described as 'not an earthly paradise, but a heavenly one.'"

Following the Shunemite

By Fr. William

From the Summer 2002 Abbey Letter

> *Let us make a small roof chamber with walls, and put there for*
> *him a bed, a table, a chair, and a lamp, so that he can stay there*
> *whenever he comes to us. (2 Kings 4:8)*

With these words, the woman of Shunem described to her husband the
guest room she wanted to build for the prophet Elisha. Add a crucifix,
an alarm clock and a wastebasket and it also describes most of the guest
rooms at St. Gregory's Abbey. There's nothing particularly surprising
about that similarity. Assuming you are talking about societies that
actually use tables, chairs, and beds, pretty much any hostess would
call these the minimum furnishings for a guestroom. Even if she lived
almost three thousand years ago.

How to furnish a simple guest room is a question with an obvious
and almost universally applicable answer. But many other questions
about the guest ministry require solutions custom made for the
particular community involved.

Chapter 53 of St. Benedict's Rule for Monasteries is titled On the
Reception of Guests. Many people are aware of its initial and central
precept, that all guests are to be welcomed as Christ himself. Not so
many have actually read and studied the entire chapter. They certainly

wouldn't be able to guess its contents by observing life as it's actually lived by the Benedictines of Three Rivers, Michigan.

The first part of Chapter 53 prescribes a great deal of high church carryings-on in the ceremonial welcoming of guests. The order is so time- and-labor- intensive that it probably was never intended to be followed each time a guest moved into the guesthouse. Today we favor a more conventional Hello or Welcome with a handshake or a hug, rather than subjecting the new arrival to an unfamiliar bit of domestic liturgy. There are people who don't want to have their feet washed by a bunch of strangers. And some would take offense on learning that we are to pray with the new guest before exchanging the kiss of peace just to make sure the guest is really a human being, and not a demon in disguise. So we don't observe these particular prescriptions of Chapter 53.

The second part of the chapter establishes the boundaries that regulate interactions between guests and monks. Here again, we at St. Gregory's have departed from St. Benedict's instructions. He permits only a few officially designated representatives of the community to speak to guests. The rest of the monks are told to respond to guests with "Bless me, please. I'm not allowed to talk to guests." Unlike the first part of the chapter, these boundaries have always been, and remain, a living tradition in parts of the Benedictine world. (This isn't as cold as it sounds. In such monasteries the monastics and guests are normally physically, as well as socially, segregated. So St. Benedict's prescribed response is almost never called for. And the officials who deal with guests are warm and concerned in their care for them.) But in our particular monastery the prohibition on conversation between guests and monks doesn't exist. In fact, the schedule includes times when the monks and guests may, and times when they practically must, socialize.

In the end, the Rule is rather spare in practical guidance on managing guest matters. Perhaps the most useful thing Chapter 53 says, after teaching us to receive all guests as Christ, is in verse 22: *Et domus Dei a sapientibus et sapienter administretur* "... and the house of God be managed by the wise and in a wise way." And that's not so useful as encouraging. It encourages any given monastery to seek the Holy Spirit's gift of wisdom in making choices concerning the monastery's guest ministry. That, in turn, means knowing something about the people who will be coming to the monastery, knowing what they are seeking and whether the monastery is the right place to seek for those things. Wise management also includes understanding what physical, personal, and financial resources are available to the community and required by different sorts of guest programs. Whether and how some things are to be done will be as obvious as the furnishings for Elisha's room. (These days it is simply not polite to wash and exorcize people before offering them a seat.) Finding the way of wisdom in other cases will require both study and experience. (When the interests of two classes of retreatants, say groups and individuals, clash; what is the best available resolution?)

This search for wisdom has led to much variety in the retreat facilities offered by different religious orders. One community might run a conference center, where a group can follow its own program and not have to coordinate with anybody else's schedule other than to show up in time for meals. Some communities provide topical retreats, where people gather to hear a particular part of the spiritual life addressed in talks by a specialist in that area. Other places offer intensive personal direction during a time of retreat, sometimes a meeting with a spiritual guide every day for holy conversation and a shared examination of what is in the retreatant's heart.

None of these, however, is what we offer at our particular monastery. When an inquirer phones or writes to ask what a retreat at St. Gregory's Abbey would involve, I explain that the most important things we have to offer to visitors are the quiet, the use of our grounds and our library, and above all the round of shared worship in the monastery church. These are things that nourish our own spiritual lives, and they are parts of the life of the monastery that we can share with our guests. A steady procession of guests indicates that these are things that many people outside the monastery are seeking.

Our own quest for wise management of the House of God includes pondering how we can best use the buildings that the kindness of our benefactors and the mercy of God have allowed us to buy or build. We want to be able to make the abbey's resources available for both group and individual retreats at the same time, rather than letting one exclude the other. And we want to be able to receive both male and female guests. Our current system for reaching these goals goes back to the fall of 1997.

On October 9th of that year, our Br. Wilfrid died in his sleep in the infirmary cell, a room adjacent to the refectory. He liked to refer to it as the death cell, although the other monks who were there before him had ended their days elsewhere, and he himself was the only one who ever really died there. Then, on the first day of November, we dedicated the new monastic dormitory, with its much improved provision for customized rooms for infirm brethren. At this point, we were in a position where the refectory was no longer in a bedroom area of the monastery. We were also confident we wouldn't have to commandeer rooms on the ground floor of St. Anthony's guesthouse to use for a sick brother and his attendants. (We had done this during Fr. Anthony's final illness.)

A new system for allotment of guest spaces, took effect January 1st, 1998. In the past, the space assigned to a retreatant had been based primarily on the sex of the retreatant. With the new system, the main criteria would be the number of retreatants in a party, and the anticipated noise level of the visit. This change increased the variety of accommodations available for both women and men.

The most visible result of this change was that St. Anthony's and the refectory were no longer exclusively male areas. (The connection between those facilities is that St. Anthony's has no kitchen and the guests staying there eat with the community.) St. Benedict's guesthouse, which had been reserved for individual women or for female or mixed groups, became available for individual men and all male groups, as well. Previously, we had not provided space for a man to come on a solitary, hermit-like retreat.

Most people are unaware of another major result of the new system. It nearly doubled the number of weekends when St. Denys is available for group retreats. Before 1998 that guesthouse served both as the main building for groups and also for individual women retreatants. The guestmaster would take care that each month at least two weekends were available for individual women, and wouldn't book group retreats for those weekends. Once we had different arrangements for individual women, or women coming in a small quiet group, we were able to make those two weekends each month available to larger groups.

Although the size of the party is normally the consideration determining which building is best for a given retreatant, other factors may be important, or even decisive. There are questions of diets that don't match the shared meals of the community, families with children, a married couple who want to be on retreat together, and the specialized concerns that go with various physical handicaps. We have dealt with these variables in different ways at different times, depending on the type of guest ministry we were trying to offer, and what guest accommodations we have available.

Just as the rooms and buildings available here for use by the guests have changed through the years and decades of our presence in Three Rivers, surely they will continue to change. So will the society in which we find ourselves and the needs of that society and the church. As they do so, we will continue to try to find the best match we can between the resources we have to offer, and the needs of those who want to spend time with us.

Here's a thought to end with. Elisha repaid the Shunemite woman's hospitality by blessing her with the gift of a son. If you have ever been blessed by our Lord during a visit to the Abbey, then pray that he will bless our monastic family with growth in numbers and holiness as well. Then come back and visit us again sometime.

Changed Perspectives
By Br. Abraham

From the Christmas 2008 Abbey Letter

The main activity here at St. Gregory's consists of public corporate prayer in the Abbey Church, and the main part of that prayer takes the form of recitation of the Psalms. Through the course of a week, the entire book of 150 Psalms is recited. That seems like a lot, and in most places it would be. In his *Rule for Monasteries,* St. Benedict laments the fact that although his monastic predecessors recited the entire Book of Psalms each day, "May we, lukewarm that we are, perform it at least in a whole week!" I do not share Benedict's grief; once a week works well for us. Many monasteries use a monthly schedule for reciting all the psalms, and others use a two-week scheme. Those schedules are good too, because they work well for them. Besides monasteries using the Book of Psalms in prayer, many churches offer public morning and evening prayer throughout the week, and most of that prayer also involves psalmody. However, most people do not live in monasteries, and most people do not live close to a church that offers daily public prayer, but many of those people still want to be involved in the psalmody going on in monasteries and churches around the world, so they adopt their own method of praying the Psalms. All in all, there are a lot of psalms read, prayed, sung, and chanted around the world every day.

Often, people who first encounter the Psalms, whether in public or private prayer or reading, find some of them surprisingly bloodthirsty. This category of psalms includes laments from the oppressed and cries for vengeance on the oppressors. Some individuals and groups simply omit these violent psalms from their prayers. Others find ways to soften these psalms by using them as analogies for inner struggles within themselves. Others deal with the brutality of the Psalms by acknowledging it for what it is; the Psalms come from a violent time (a good reminder of the violent brutality of our own society). The competing empires and kingdoms of the Iron Age from which the Psalms come were made of real people who really prayed, and even if our understanding of God has changed and become less vengeful and ethnocentric, we can still use their prayers as bases for our own. We can also use them as prods to see if our understanding of God really is less vengeful and ethnocentric than Iron Age attitudes.

With experience, most people find ways to pray the psalms that express the laments of the oppressed, because even if they are not being oppressed at the time, they can pray with and for all those around the world who are suffering. That is how I approach these psalms. I had

a wonderful childhood surrounded by people who loved me, and as a middle class American I am one of the richest persons in the world with the best in medical care and educational opportunities at my fingertips. Even as a monk who has no personal possessions, my community provides me with all I could need, and more than I should want. So I pray the psalms of lament for all those around the world whom I read about in the newspaper or see on news broadcasts that are suffering from natural or manmade disasters. Even when I am feeling slightly oppressed by others or by work waiting to be done, these psalms serve to remind me of how good my life really is and how I need to stop whining.

The discomfort occurs when the psalmists ask God to bring disaster on the oppressors. Such an attitude does not fit well with our call to go the extra mile, turn the other cheek, and charitably bless those who hate us. Perhaps the most famous examples of cursing in the Psalms occur in what are otherwise considered by some to be two of the most beautiful songs in the world: Psalm 137, in which homesick exiles explain how they have put away their musical instruments because they are too heartbroken to sing anymore; and Psalm 139, in which a poet expresses wonderment at his own being and amazement at God's infinite nature. Yet near the end of both of these, bloody curses are added: the homesick exiles bless anyone who will dash their oppressors' children on the rocks, and the poet declares his hatred for those who do not share his attitudes toward God. These examples are only two of many such curses interspersed throughout the Psalter. Some other psalms seem to be an almost unbroken stream of hateful desires and hopes for retribution upon enemies, and it is not surprising that many people find them difficult to pray.

I have found a way to use the cursing psalms as an aid to foster my own prayer. It might not be the most proper use of these psalms, but so far it has helped me, and maybe that in itself makes it a proper use. When one of these bloodthirsty verses comes up as we pray in the monastery church, I remind myself that I am not the innocent person cursing the sinner; I am the sinner making life miserable for the people around me. I need to change. I need to ask not only for forgiveness, but also for the strength to repent — to really change and make the love of

God the center of my life rather than keeping myself in that position. The people I come in contact with everyday are the psalmists crying out for deliverance from the oppression I bring them because of my selfishness. I cause them to sin by driving them to curse me.

This realization of my own oppressive behavior does not derive from an overly scrupulous sense of unworthiness. I am a beautiful Child of God created to love and be loved, just like everyone else. But I have allowed my own pettiness to hurt myself and the people around me. I am not the only one who is guilty of this. The tiny, daily misdemeanors we all commit in order to get what we want when we want it are not fair to anyone, including ourselves. Knowing this should not drive us to despair. Rather, it should prompt a firm resolve to change, knowing that even though only God can transform us, only we as individuals can allow God to do that, and only we can purposefully use the gifts that God has given us as tools to change. We are worth the effort it takes to grow into the mature individuals we are created to be.

Changing one's perspective from oppressed to oppressor might not help everyone pray these psalms as it has helped me, but that's OK. It is good to heed the advice to pray as we can, not as we can't. Maybe the one thing to avoid is putting ourselves in the position of God and presuming that it is our right to carry out the curses.

Let us Bow and Bend Low

By Fr. Jude

From the Fall 2003 Abbey Letter

In Chapter 9 of his Rule for Monasteries, St. Benedict writes:

> As soon as the cantor begins to sing Glory be to the
> Father, let all the monks rise from their seats in honor
> and reverence for the Holy Trinity.

It would be convenient if St. Benedict had gone on to tell us monks just what to do once we had risen. But he did not tell us, so we at St. Gregory's follow the usual Benedictine tradition of bowing, not just bowing but bowing *profoundly*, during the naming of the three Persons of the Holy Trinity.

The profound bow startled me when I first saw it on a visit to St. Gregory's in 1950. But one expects to find monks doing odd things; and I soon got used to the extravagance of the monks' standing up at the end of every psalm and bowing over so far that their heads were about on a level with their waistlines. The rule of thumb is that one bows far enough to place the palms of the hands on the kneecaps. That's about as far as a bow can go. Such a bow is found mainly in monasteries, though in other places a profound bow rather than a genuflexion is the usual reverence paid to the Blessed Sacrament.

Bowing is not something that we do only in church. Various degrees of bowing are common in our secular society, although we don't come near to the formalized systems of bowing found in some far eastern cultures. Perhaps the simplest form of the bow often used among us is the *nod*, the movement mainly of the head, by which we signal to an acquaintance on the far side of a crowded reception room or a few rows away at the theater that we see them, although we are too far away to speak. The nod can be friendly and welcoming or it can be cold and dismissive, depending on the facial expression accompanying it. In any case, it is an acknowledgment of someone's presence. The minimal bow can also be used to acknowledge that you hear what someone is saying but have no wish to reply. In *Pride and Prejudice*, when a remark of Mr. Darcy's touched on an awkward subject, Elizabeth answered only by a slight bow.

More communicative is the kind of bow one makes if the emcee at a banquet or the chairman at a meeting says, We're honored to have so-and-so with us tonight, and motions for so-and-so to stand. So-and-so takes a bow, as we say, nodding and maybe putting the shoulders a bit into it, to indicate appreciation of being noticed, or pleasure in being there, or something of the sort.

And then there is the curtain call after a successful performance, when the bow says Thank you to the applause of the audience. I'm pleased that you liked what I did. This bow can be just as extravagant in its way as the monks' profound bow, depending on the nature of the applause and the inclination of the performer. Bravas may bring forth deep curtseys and blown kisses, loud bravos a hand on the heart and an embrace-like motion of open arms.

The bow can express a variety of other human responses. It goes with obedience; the butler bows to show his acceptance of your request for brandy and cigars in the den. Monks bow (not profoundly) to one another when they enter or leave the monastic choir stalls in the course of a formal procession, bespeaking the injunction of the Rule to vie in paying obedience one to another. The bowed head goes with an apology and request for pardon. And a bow from the waist is a physical necessity for a man who shakes the hand of a seated woman, and in this case adds a note of respect.

Everything that a bow can express is summed up to the ultimate degree in the monk's profound bow: acknowledgment of the presence of Another, appreciation for being noticed, gratitude for being loved, sorrow for offenses, the promise of future obedience. And these thoughts carry beyond their humanly social meaning. Obedience moves on to submission, apology to contrition, respect to adoration. If the monk can match his inner disposition to the outward movement of the profound bow, then the physical act becomes rich spiritual nourishment.

The profound bow is disabling. With the back bent and the eyes properly lowered, you can see only the floor of the monastic choir and some feet. You may see the edge of the desk of your choir stall, but it's so close to your nose that the text of an open book lying there is only a blur. You are also defenseless. The structure of your choir stall offers some protection, but a frontal attack by someone with a baseball bat could be damaging. (I've never heard of any monk being subject to such an assault, but it is a possibility, however remote.) Powerless and vulnerable, we take our true stance before our Maker. It's a moment of truth.

The profound bow is not for everyone everywhere. It would be odd, out of place, either at worship in a parish church or while saying grace at dinner at home. Monks do not indulge in the profound bow outside of the monastery church; it is not part of the mealtime ritual in the monastic refectory. But fitted into the *Opus Dei*, the Work of God (St. Benedict's name for the divine office), it serves as a reminder of what the Christian's posture before God ought to be. If it is accompanied by a movement of the will and an act of recollection, it is a grace-bringing moment of worship. But you don't have to bow. Every Christian can, anytime, anywhere, offer to the Father, the Son, and the Holy Spirit what the profound bow symbolizes—the intellect's moment of recollection and the will's turning toward love.

On Disinterested Reading

By Abbot Andrew

From the Fall 2004 Abbey Letter

In February 2004, I attended the American Abbots' Workshop, as I do almost every year. Our speaker this time was Michael Casey, a Cistercian monk from Australia, who has written several excellent books on monastic spirituality. In an engaging series of talks saturated with his calm yet ardent thirst for God, he discussed ten commandments for those living the monastic life, which he extracted from St. Benedict's Rule for Monasteries. One of the commandments, taken from the fourth verse of Chapter 48, states that we should devote ourselves to reading. It is instructive that the title of Chapter 48 is The Daily Manual Labor. More instructive still, although Benedict outlines the times of day when manual work should be done, this chapter says far more about reading than it does about work. The implication of this chapter, then, is that reading is not an optional pastime, but is an intrinsic part of a life of service to God and neighbor.

Most likely, Benedict himself

expected this reading to consist primarily of Holy Scripture and the writings of the Fathers such as Saint Basil and John Cassian. Tapping into much monastic experience over the centuries, however, Michael Casey spoke of reading as an engagement in generalized culture, that is, exploring many areas of intellectual and personal interest. This engagement with generalized culture requires leisure. Michael Casey defined leisure as freedom from external constraints; the sphere of the fully human. Leisure provides scope for expression of the deep self in play, wisdom, creative work, contemplation, art, friendship and kindness. Just as leisure creates space for ourselves to broaden our lives, the enemies of leisure that Casey listed: obsession, ambition, overwork, sloth and escapism shrink and narrow our lives.

The phrase that Michael Casey used to describe the practice of leisurely reading was "disinterested reading." Those words rang a loud bell for me, because that is precisely the same phrase that my novice master Father Anthony used. The use of the word "disinterested" may be startling, because nowadays it is often used to mean "not interested," but the American Heritage Dictionary appends a note to the definition of this word, insisting that the meaning of "unbiased, free of self-interest" is much the more proper meaning of the word. The Oxford English Dictionary includes the attractive definition: "free from self-seeking."

Although neither Michael Casey nor Father Anthony defined this term, I think I am close to what they were getting at, as well as faithful to the proper meaning of the word, if I define disinterested reading as reading without a specific agenda. It is this lack of an agenda that frees reading from constraints and allows for a leisurely play in the activity. The freedom from self-seeking both prevents this activity of reading from becoming egocentric and deepens the formative effect on the reader.

Reading a book for a specific purpose may also be enjoyable, of course, but it is not an act of leisure. Here it helps to note the formative effect of the prayerful reading of scripture, a practice that builds the foundation for all other reading. There are times when I have to study portions of scripture for a specific purpose, such as preparing a sermon. The result of this intentional effort is often rewarded by insights that might not have come without that effort. However, most of my prayerful reading of scripture is done disinterestedly; that is, without trying to accomplish anything beyond spending time with God and with God's Word. Over the years, the conviction has grown in me that it is reading without trying to accomplish anything in particular that has allowed God's Word to sink deeply into my whole being.

In discussing the leisure of which disinterested reading is an embodiment, Michael Casey noted that leisure allows us to have time not to be busy, and this non-busy time gives us time to listen to one another. That thought has given me the idea that reading is an act of hospitality towards the writer, an act that welcomes someone into our lives. We listen to other people most deeply and are thus most hospitable to them when we do not have an agenda concerning them. The same is true with the author of a book that we have invited to come and speak to us. Such listening is a quality I saw in Father Anthony again and again over the years.

This act of listening has in itself a formative value for us, one that can benefit the people who enter into our lives. As we listen to a writer, we have the opportunity to try out new ideas and alternate ways of living. Some of these ideas and ways of living will seem impractical and in some cases even seriously wrong, but other ideas and visions

of living differently can spur us on to doing things that change the world. It is the disinterested quality that allows us to toy with these ideas without being too anxious about them. But then, once an idea has really grabbed our interest, our actions can be focused and full of interest in other people.

Such listening also requires reading at a pace slow enough to engage in conversation with the author. Speed-reading has its place for those who can do it, but disinterested reading is not that place. Rather, Michael Casey recommends a leisurely pace of reading that exchanges instant gratification for long-term delight and which fosters a slow intellectual metabolism.

In listing some of the benefits of disinterested reading, Michael Casey notes that this practice facilitates a reflective, substantial life. It also broadens and refines the mind so as to give us a wider context to our own experience that adds depth to our beliefs and values. The little game of trying out new ideas and alternate ways of living makes no sense if we do not have any core convictions of our own to give us a frame of reference for the thought experiments we are invited to try. Our convictions might change as a result of some of these experiments but these changes won't be impulsive. Rather, these changes will be the result of much listening and thinking. On the other hand, many times the result of these experiments will be to confirm and thus deepen the convictions which we brought to the book in the first place. It is when our convictions are regularly tested through the challenges of listening and imagining possibilities that our convictions can be most focused without our needing to use them as weapons with which to bludgeon people we don't agree with. There are some movies that can foster a reflective response and, theoretically, television could do the same. Unfortunately, much of the entertainment industry seems to be designed to close off leisurely thought rather than provide space for it. On the other side of the coin, it is the authors who eschew the sledgehammer and communicate most thoughtfully who are easiest to listen to and be challenged by.

The actual books one might read disinterestedly will, of course, differ from person to person. Because theology books and other books on Christianity interest me, I read these books along with books on numerous other subjects that help put my faith in context. This sort of broad-ranging reading seems to be what Michael Casey is recommending to us, and it certainly was true of Fr. Anthony's reading habits. It is worth noting that C. S. Lewis, in his essay "On Stories," stressed the importance of being a good reader much more than he emphasized reading the best books. That is to say, one who reads even inferior literature hospitably and experimentally will get more out of reading than one who reads great books with a closed mind and heart. In my experience, many books considered to be light reading have given me much to think about. I will add, however, that I don't get much delight from any book that doesn't give me some sustenance mentally and spiritually.

Not everybody finds reading all that helpful in cultivating holy leisure. Benedict himself realized this and at the end of this same chapter on work and reading, he suggests that such people be given a type of work or craft that will keep them busy without overwhelming them. It happens that the Abbot Primate of the Benedictine Confederation, Notker Wolf, was at this workshop and, although himself a man of highly cultured intellect, he brought up this verse during our discussion. Clearly the Abbot Primate wants us to be open and flexible to other experiences of holy leisure besides those which come with reading. Benedict's example of practicing a handicraft is a particularly good one since this sort of activity can accomplish many of the same objectives as disinterested reading does.

Just as people possess various abilities for reading, people have different amounts of time available for the practice of disinterested reading. A major part of the discipline of reading is to carve out time for it in the face of many obstacles, which can exist even in a monastery. This discipline also entails making use of small amounts of time that are available. Fr. Anthony was a great master of that practice. These short periods of time add up to a lot of reading and they leaven the whole day with the sense of leisure that helps us listen to God and neighbor.

It is important to remember that some of the obstacles to disinterested reading are within ourselves. Michael Casey listed ambition and overwork among the enemies of leisure. When we are not only possessed by these enemies of leisure but also have social and economic power, we hurt not only ourselves, but also many other people by engulfing them in our own ambition. The effects of this problem are all around us throughout the world. This is all the more reason for each of us to engage in disinterested reading so that we can playfully yet earnestly imagine new ways we can live together, free to engage in holy leisure.

Friends of God: A Sermon on St Benedict's Day

By Br. Abraham

From the Summer 2000 Abbey Letter

Genesis 12: 1-4a; Ephesians 3: 14-19; John 15: 9-17

We are God's friends. We just heard Jesus say in today's Gospel: "I do not call you servants any longer...I have called you friends...." It is good to be with friends. When we are with friends, we can be ourselves without worrying about appearances. We can do ordinary, everyday things and find great satisfaction in them: sitting on the couch, riding around in the car with no particular destination, goofing off at work, talking about silly or stupid things, or maybe not talking at all. Friendships thrive on the ordinary, everyday things in life, not on the spectacular. Spectacular things may happen; but they cannot be the basis of friendship, because spectacles don't last, and neither do those things based upon them.

And our friendship with God is meant to last. Right before Jesus calls his disciples friends, he says "Abide in my love." Right after he calls them friends, he tells them to bear fruit, fruit that will last. Both abiding and bearing fruit take time and require stability. They can't

be rushed, and they involve a lot of unspectacular, everyday work. We might not think of abiding as taking a lot of work, but just think of all the people you know who can't sit still for five minutes, much less keep the same address for a year or two. We might have a fuller concept of the labor involved in bearing fruit from growing a summer garden or, better, from planting and tending an orchard or vineyard. Abiding in God's love and bearing fruit are much the same: they take a lot of work, patience, fortitude, and time. They might not be the most glamorous things to do, but they are what God our friend has asked of us.

We heard Paul writing to the Ephesians about abiding and bearing fruit when he prays that they may be strengthened in their inner being...and that Christ may dwell in their hearts...as they are being rooted and grounded in love. All of that suggests a lengthy process, not a one-shot emotional or spiritual rocket to heaven. Rockets may go off every now and then, but they are not necessary, because heaven is not a place we need to get to—heaven is a place we need to cultivate and abide in. If we abide in Jesus, and allow him to abide in us, then heaven can and should be wherever we are, and that is why we need to work so patiently to bring it to fruition.

We bring heaven to our world in simple ways; making God's love a concrete thing for those around us. A TV preacher once said an unusually smart thing by commenting that people don't make love in bed, they celebrate love in bed. Love is made earlier in the day by cooking, cleaning, and earning a living. That's what we should do as God's friends—at home, at work, in the monastery or at our parish—making love for and with others by doing our simple, daily round of chores in peace and joy, thereby slowly and surely helping to bring heaven to those around us. Every once in a while we might have the chance to do something spectacular, and of course we should do the best we can when that happens, but we shouldn't be disappointed if the opportunity never occurs. As Mother Teresa of Calcutta said, "We don't need to do big things, we only need to do the little things with love." The big things might seem more important and heroic, but in the end they are much easier than the little things, because the little, everyday, ordinary things never end, and they can easily become drudgery if not done in thoughtfulness and love.

The story of Abram which we heard today is a good example of patiently abiding and bearing fruit. It may sound strange to say that a man who spent his entire adult life wandering around the Middle East is a good example of patiently abiding; but Abram's home was in God, no matter where he pitched his tent. Abram lived in God's promise through good times and bad, through doubt and surprise, and because of his constancy, produced fruit that is still blessing the world. A lot of spectacular things happened while Abram traveled (including having his name changed to Abraham), and we read about them to help us in our life with God, but it was the ordinary, everyday work that made those big things possible: pulling down the tents, setting them up again, grazing and watering the flocks, finding suitable places to camp, calming family disputes. That's a lot of hard work, even with all his slaves. We should be thankful for his work and patience, and we should follow his example.

And so today, in that spirit, we remember one of God's most unspectacular of saints—Benedict. He is not a popular figure. When people look for an icon or medal bearing his image, they usually have to search through pages of catalogues filled with pictures and stories of several other more glamorous saints, and even then are lucky to find anything in his memory. However, the work that he did in setting forth a way of life based on patiently abiding in Christ and bearing fruit from that relationship has had long-term effects that most of those other more popular figures can't claim. We should be thankful for his work and patience, and follow his example, bringing God's love to our world as best we can in our own time and place with joy, constancy, and peace. And now in his memory and honor as we continue our festival of the mundane, let us with thankful and ordinary, everyday hearts prepare to meet at this familiar table for yet one more meal with the God who calls us friend.

Nothing is to Be Preferred to the Work of God

By Prior Aelred

From the Easter 2011 Abbey Letter

It seems that ever since St. Gregory's Abbey adopted the vernacular for the recitation of the Daily Office in November of 1967, we have been in the process of revision. With the adoption of English there has been the question of what translation to use. Then there has been the question of what liturgical materials are available. Some have questioned the appropriateness of certain psalms and canticles for Christian use. The issue of inclusive language has raised another question.

As I am supposedly overseeing the current process of revision, it seemed that some reflections of the Daily Office, its history, what it has meant to Benedictines and to the monks of St. Gregory's would be apt.

When the early monks referred to the Work of God they meant the entire practice of the monastic life with its attendant vigils, fasts and manual labor, but in chapter XLIII of the Rule of Our Holy Father Benedict when it states, nothing is to be preferred to the Work of God, it is the performance of the Daily Office that is meant. A change had occurred in the course of the intervening centuries.

Exactly how such a change came about is a thorny question. Such evidence as exists is sufficient to permit the adoption of different points of view but slight enough to preclude consensus. It seems likely that the change is at least partly a result of the performance of the Daily Office ceasing to be part of the normal life of the average Christian and being seen as the task of the religious professionals. Exactly why this should have occurred is also unclear. In the Latin Church it would be tempting to speculate that the prayer of the church being in a language "not understanded of the people" would make the laity less inclined to participate. Unfortunately for this suggestion, a similar change also occurred in the Greek Church (where the language of the prayer of the church and the vernacular remained the same) as well as the fact that it occurred in the west before the development of vernacular languages other than Latin (it is worth keeping in mind that the vernacular of Benedict and his monks was Latin). It also seems true that Cranmer anticipated the adoption of the Book of Common Prayer would lead to

the laity in the parishes performing Morning and Evening Prayer in the place of the Divine Office previously chanted by the monks and nuns of the suppressed monasteries. Regardless of what explanations there might be of the disappearance of lay participation in the Daily Office, it is indisputable that in all these cases the celebration of the Daily Office was no longer a component of the normal life of the average Christian but became instead part of the duty of the religious professionals (of all the churches influenced by the Reformation it seems that the Church of England was the only one which continued to require the recitation of the Daily Office by the clergy).

One possible solution to this development is that the Daily Office as it came to be performed in cathedrals ceased to meet the religious needs of the laity for other reasons than being in a foreign tongue. This explanation requires some knowledge of the historical background of the Daily Office once again bearing in mind that the evidence is meager and subject to differing interpretations.

From the beginnings of the monastic life, whether eremetical or cenobitic, repetition of passages of Sacred Scripture, especially the psalms, was an essential aspect of the life. The primary purpose, even in cenobitic communities or when the hermits gathered to pray together, was individual and ascetic. The goal was to put on the mind of Christ by immersing oneself in the Word of God. Since it was assumed that God had something important to communicate in every word, it followed that all parts of Scripture (included some works that were not included in the canon eventually established, such as the Shepherd of Hermas and the Letter of Barnabas) were used. From early descriptions it seems that the monks took turns offering some passage from Scripture. This was followed by a period of silence while all pondered its significance. After the silence the leader would say a prayer that collected all of the prayers of the individual participants (hence the word, collect). At some early time the psalms were recognized as being especially appropriate for this form of common prayer which, combined with the desire to include all of the Word of God, led to some arrangement of the entire Psalter being prayed through in some period of time (in the Holy Rule it is specified that the entire Psalter should be prayed through each week). There is considerable disagreement as to how often the early monks gathered for such prayer, but in cenobitic communities the entire group seems to have assembled at the beginning and close of the day. The emphasis on personal edification and complete use of Scripture has led liturgists to describe forms of the Daily Office of this type as monastic.

A different approach to prayer in common developed outside the monasteries and became popular in cathedrals and basilicas. Again the times for assembly were typically at the beginning and close of the day, but the approach was quite different. The emphasis was on corporate praise, celebration and intercession. Rather than all of the Psalter being recited on some sort of schedule, only certain psalms appropriate to the time of day or the occasion being celebrated were used. Readings from Scripture were brief or sometimes (apparently) dispensed with entirely. Modern liturgists have coined the term cathedral office for this form of the Daily Office.

One might assume that a monastic office was prayed here at St. Gregory's and other monasteries and that a cathedral office was prayed in cathedrals and parishes that prayed the Daily Office (using, perhaps, the Book of Common Prayer). Alas, the situation is not so simple. It was already most complex and mixed by the time that the so called Liturgical Code was composed for the Holy Rule.

The Holy Rule sets out a scheme of eight times in each day when the monks are to assemble for common prayer. The rationale is set forth in chapter XVI, "The Prophet says: 'Seven times a day I have praised you.' We will fulfill this sacred number of seven if we satisfy our obligations of service at Lauds, Prime, Terce, Sext, None, Vespers and Compline, for it was of these hours that he said: 'Seven times a day I have praised you.' Concerning Vigils, the same Prophet says: 'At midnight I arose to give you praise.' Therefore, we should praise our Creator for his just judgments at these times: Lauds, Prime, Terce, Sext, None, Vespers and Compline; and let us arise at night to give him praise."

For centuries monks prayed a form of the Divine Office that was unchanged, except for the occasional addition of a new feast, but after the reforms of the Second Vatican Council, everything changed. It is a complicated story and some descriptions and reflections will need another article.

Hobbies at the Monastery
From the Fall 2008 Abbey Letter

Life at St. Gregory's is centered around public prayer times in the abbey church. In addition to corporate prayer, the monks are expected to spend time in private prayer and scripture reading every day. We also spend several hours each day on chores involving the upkeep of our grounds and buildings, driving guests to and from public transportation sites, preparation for occasional outside ministry, and correspondence with people who write to us with various questions. Add all of that time together with time spent setting tables, gathering for meals, washing up after meals, bathing, and sleeping, and not much is left for personal interests and hobbies.

Yet we do find time every now and then to engage in favorite interests. St. Gregory's has a good library, music practice room, and music listening room, as well as a selection of video tapes and discs, and so we can often be found spending free time reading, listening to music, or watching a movie. One might ask why monks should even indulge in leisure activities that might take their minds off of God, but a wise monk knows that one of the best forms of prayer and thanksgiving is that of simply enjoying the wonderful world that God has given us. We also know that leisure activities can threaten to become substitutes for prayer or demand too much of our attention during prayer times, and so we must always be aware of our activities and do them in such a way that they foster prayer, rather than hinder it.

With all of that said, we thought it might be of interest to our readers to have some of our monks describe their favorite hobbies:

Br. Martin

After entering the monastery, I became attracted to the use of paper in various artistic ways. As correspondence with an increasing number of people began to develop, I started to make greeting cards in one form or another. These were meant to be both a creative outlet for me, and an encouraging treat within my letters. At first I tried my hand in making pop-up cards. Not only was this fun, but it was also challenging, since I had to work out the mechanics of a successful pop-up.

Currently I work with art rubber stamps to make cards, bookmarks, and stationery. Rubber stamps enable me to use various images to illustrate spiritual truths that are important to me. It also allows me to work with color, since I kept my pop-up cards simple and monochromatic. I find making cards not only enjoyable, but also a good learning experience, not merely in learning new techniques, but mainly in teaching me how to focus on a particular thing and forget about myself for awhile. This is important to me as I strive to not be so self-centered but more focused on God.

Br. Abraham

When I first entered the monastery, I spent a lot of time playing and listening to music. I even gave a recital at the monastery and at a local community college (putting my music degree in bassoon performance to good use). I also wrote a lot of music, knowing full well that I would probably never hear any of it performed, since most of it involved large ensembles. I was OK with that, and can look at a shelf full of my own symphonies with contentment, simply because I know that I enjoy them when I play them in my head. I purposely stopped writing music a few years ago because it took so much time and energy and was pulling at my attention during prayer and work time.

Now I spend much of my free time riding a bicycle on the roads surrounding the monastery. I have several routes ranging from ten to forty miles, depending on the amount of time there is before I need to be home. I picked up this hobby from a friend with whom I took a bike trip down the West Coast the summer before I entered the monastery, and have enjoyed it ever since. I even took a bike trip a few years ago across Wisconsin with Fr. Gregory, OJN, the superior of the Order f Julian of Norwich at the time. Another hobby of mine involving wheels is that of following IndyCar racing. Occasionally I get a chance to watch televised races in addition to reading about them in the newspaper and online. I have even had a few opportunities to attend races in person at a few speedways, and have greatly enjoyed each opportunity. I am slowly learning to be grateful not only for the cars on the track, but also for each of the tens of thousands of individuals in the stands, even the obnoxious ones — a great way to grow in prayer.

Br. Cuthbert

One of my earliest discoveries upon joining the monastery was that we had a large amount of brewing equipment in the basement. It seems that some of the monks of long ago had an interest in brewing, and their tools were kept in the basement to collect dust and await someone else who might want to make an attempt at it. Knowing a bit about the history of monks making beer (a tradition dating back well over a thousand years) and having an interest in the brewing process myself, I decided to try my hand at it in the hope that I had inherited the monkish knack for making good beer. After a few experimental small scale batches that were rather disappointing, I took the plunge and brewed a five gallon batch that turned out really well. That was about three years ago, and ever since I have been brewing beer that is generally well received. We only drink it on Sundays and solemnities, though often that depends on whether I have had the time to brew something ahead of time.

Being the cook, brewing dovetails quite well with my other duties and provides an opportunity to spend enjoyable time in the kitchen that is more than simply 'work.' The beer making process itself—from brewing to bottling—is fascinating to me, as many of our guests have learned when they ask about the beer. Some guests have even suggested that we should start selling the beer, which I take as a compliment, but there are a whole host of reasons why that will likely never happen; not least among which is the extra work it would create for everyone else in the monastery. So the hobby will remain just a hobby, though my hope is that it will continue to surprise and delight everyone who has a chance to enjoy the fruit of what I like to think of as 'leisurely labor.'

My other hobby is making 3-D paper models. Most of what I do comes in the form of kits (pre-printed booklets where one has to score, cut, fold, and glue together the different pieces) although I have been known to draw and build a few things from scratch. Most of the models I have made are of cathedrals or other houses of worship. There are a few examples of my handiwork in different places in the monastery, the most public of which is in the library on top of the card catalogue. Much like brewing beer, patience and attention to detail are important in paper modeling, but the final products of both are quite different. After all, one can't drink a model cathedral!

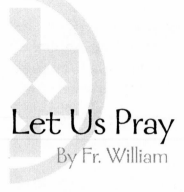

Let Us Pray
By Fr. William

From the Summer 2009 Abbey Letter

An annual phenomenon I've learned about since I've been guestmaster here at St. Gregory's Abbey is the August rush. I wasn't aware of it before I had this job, but I've been assured that the monks who were guestmasters before me all noticed it too. Each year in August there's a big increase in the number of people asking to come to the monastery for a time of retreat.

Now, August isn't actually the most comfortable time to visit the Abbey. The guesthouses here aren't air conditioned. We have our share (and more) of bloodsucking insects at that time of year. That month doesn't offer the soft greens and flowers of spring, or the good walking weather and colored leaves of autumn. But the August rush comes each year, just the same.

What happens is this: as the warm months approach, people decide to make the time to go on retreat this summer. But those plans never quite become solid enough to act on. Then, all of a sudden, August is upon us, and as Jeremiah says, Summer is ended and we are not saved. So folks rush to the phone and the e-mail to set something up while there's still a bit of time to act on their good intentions. I don't suppose this should be surprising. Summer rivals New Year's Day as a time of high minded plans, and good intentions: put a deck on the back of the house, read *Don Quixote*, landscape the front yard, stop smoking, re-learn whatever foreign language one studied back in the day.

Here's a summer project I'd like to offer for people's consideration: start praying every day. There are a lot of Christians who just get out of the habit of praying regularly as they grow up. They're not *against* prayer. It's just not something they do on their own, unless there's a crisis or perhaps a really glorious sunset, or piece of music that moves them to address their comments to God. Often what has happened is that they outgrew the prayers they used to say as children, but never found an adult replacement for those devotions.

That's a pity, because daily prayer serves several important functions in the life of a follower of Jesus. Most obviously, it is a way of our staying in touch with God. God is always with us, of course. But for that fact to have meaning in our lives, we need to make an explicit recognition of God's presence, and prayer does that. But this recognition isn't the only thing going on in prayer. We actually say things when we pray, praising the Lord, and bringing our concerns to the One who cares for us.

Daily prayer is also a sign that we are serious in our commitment to our faith. This isn't to say that Christians who don't engage in daily prayer don't believe in God, or that they don't love God. But our practice of prayer is one of the ways that other people, whether followers of other faiths, or people of no faith at all, can recognize that we not

only identify with a particular religion, but we do something about and with that religion as a part of our everyday lives. Regular prayer is a part of living out our response to the gospel of Jesus Christ.

People who would like to regain this enriching element of the Christian life need to give it a bit of thought and planning, and then just jump in and do it. That's not too demanding as summer projects go. It doesn't take nearly as much planning as the deck on the back of the house, and when you travel or move, you take your prayer with you. So it's really a pretty good deal. The first bit of planning is simply settling the question of whether your daily prayers are an individual effort, or a time of family devotions. For the rest of this article, I'll focus on individual prayer.

Next, you have to set aside a time for your daily prayers. The time doesn't have to be expressed in terms of morning prayers at seven o'clock. Something like between my shower and breakfast should work fine, if your shower and breakfast are regular items in your daily routine. And devotions don't have to be the same time every day. If your Wednesday and Thursday schedules are different from the rest of the week, then your prayers would reasonably come at a different time on those days. But scheduling is important. Prayer is like exercise or homework, if it's going to be done, it should have a dedicated time, and be done regularly. Remember those folks who were going to go on retreat sometime during the summer. And remember what happened to the homework that was going to be done when we got around to it.

For individual prayer, I'd suggest twice a day, morning and evening. There are several reasons for this. Somebody who can't see a way to carve out a ten minute slot for prayer can probably figure out some way to make two five minute times. And someone for whom twenty minutes would be unthinkable may be able to manage two ten minute times. Furthermore, turning to the Lord in prayer at both the start and end of the day has a spiritual healthiness to it. It gives the opportunity to make our prayer balanced and integrated with the rhythms of our life that once a day prayer doesn't.

So once you've decided when to pray, you choose how to pray. This is much a matter of personal preference. Some people may want to offer entire church services on their own every day. But most folks who have drifted away from daily prayer and are trying to get back into the habit of it probably want something simpler, more personal, and briefer. So here are a few suggestions with those folks in mind.

To start off, take time for deliberately entering into the presence of God. Most of the time that means mentally stepping back from worldly concerns and recalling that you are addressing yourself to your Lord. Seeking out some quiet and closing your eyes will probably be a help. This is the mental equivalent to entering some private sacred chapel for our time of devotion. If you're praying in front of a favorite sacred symbol, or at some particularly moving place (remember that sunset?), take time to move through the symbol to the God it's meant to bring you nearer to.

Morning is a good time for prayers of praise, thanks and dedication. After all, the Lord has brought you through the night alive and the sun has risen one more time, so praise the Lord for all the blessings showered on us. And ask God's blessing and guidance and protection through the day ahead. The evening is a traditional time for self-examination and confession, since we hope we're through with most of our sinning for the day. And we thank God for particular favors during the day just past.

What many people think of when they hear the word prayer is petition and intercession. These are the prayers that ask God's assistance and blessing and favors for ourselves and others. We can do this at either or both of our prayer times. But I expect you'll find that either morning or evening offers a longer period for you to spend in prayer, and you'll discover your petitions and intercessions tend to settle into the longer session.

It may be a good thing to mix prayer in your own words with prayers from other sources. For some people this means using a daily devotional guide. Others will like to use favorite set forms for things like confession and general thanksgiving or praise. But if speaking your mind in your own way suits you best, you can stick with that. Since the Lord's Prayer is a gift to us from Jesus himself, including that is a blessing on its own. So you may want to include that even if you don't use other set forms. And if you're in a setting where you wouldn't be disturbing other people, don't be afraid to sing if you want to. A favorite hymn or chant isn't at all out of place in personal prayer.

Some people will want to include some Bible reading with their daily prayers. This is a good thing, of course. But if you are just starting out and only have a little time for your daily prayer, then it may be a better idea to separate prayer time and Bible time. Praying regularly, even for a little while, is very important in developing the habit of prayer. That's not the important thing in reading the Bible. In reading the Holy Scriptures, the important thing is to understand what we are reading, and to allow the Word to work on us. To do that we need to have time to hear an integral piece of the text and to understand what it's saying. And if we have reference materials to help us, that's even better. Trying to fit that into part of a brief prayer time won't work. Reading with understanding in heart and mind are what we should be working for. So rather than trying to squeeze that into an already brief prayer time, look for a time or two during the week when you can really sit down and read a whole story or psalm or prophecy, and understand what it's saying.

Of course, you don't have to stick with those little baby-step bits of time for your morning and evening prayer. As you settle into the habit of daily prayer, you'll probably find that time available for your conversations with the Lord becomes more ample. And maybe you'll decide to use that extra time to see what God has to say to you through the Scriptures, or you may want to spend more time in quiet wordless communion with Jesus, the lover of your soul, or maybe you'll find you're the chatty type, who simply has more to say than you did at the beginning. In any case, don't be afraid to grow in your adventure of daily prayer.

Across the Universe
by Br. Abraham

From the Easter 2007 Abbey Letter

The main activity at St. Gregory's Abbey consists of public corporate prayer in the Abbey Church, and the main part of that prayer takes the form of recitation of the Psalms. On a normal day, we gather together seven times for communal prayer, beginning at four in the morning for the office of Matins and continuing at intervals throughout the day for the other offices of Lauds, Terce, Sext, None, Vespers, and Compline. (The term office comes from the Latin words *opus*, meaning work, and *officium*, meaning duty, obligation, or service. The names of the various offices come from Latin terms that hint at either the time of day at which the certain office is performed or at some of the psalms used in that office.) Through the course of a week, the entire book of 150 Psalms is recited. Some psalms are used only once; others are used several times a week or even every day.

Although some special days and holidays utilize certain psalms reflecting the mood of the day, most often we simply recite them in order of their appearance in the Psalter. Even on those special days that are given particular psalms, we do not recite them at all offices that day; most of the offices for those days still use the psalms assigned for that day of the week. This schedule causes us to recite seemingly inappropriate psalms sometimes: happy ones on solemn fasts, and sad ones on happy feasts. It also means that at any time of day, a particular monk might be reciting a psalm that does not match his mood at the time. While that can be distressing for someone not used to it, it has become a great comfort for many people throughout history. It reminds us that our situations and feelings are not permanent; the psalms sung at Friday Sext might not fit a particular monk's concerns this week, but they might perfectly meet the needs of the monk next to him or of one of the guests in the church, and they might coincide with his own next week. It also reminds us that the prayer is not all about the individual. Corporate prayer is corporate prayer, not private prayer (there are times of day set aside for private prayer).

In a way, all prayer is corporate prayer, even private meditation and scripture reading. Since each Christian is a part of the Body of Christ, everything done by one affects all the others. All Christians at prayer make up the Body of Christ praying with and for the entire

world. We are united throughout space and time by the Holy Spirit praying through us, and since the Spirit of God is infinite, imminent, and transcendent, true prayer reflects those qualities. We as individuals are important, but no more or less than all other individuals. One might even say that as children of God with the Holy Spirit filling us and binding us together, we are all infinitely important. So while our prayer should not be completely dictated by our individual desires, all of our needs and wants (real or imagined) are addressed by all prayers around the world: past, present, and future.

In a way, it is not even we who are praying, since it is the Holy Spirit who is praying through us. Our perspective is so tiny that we can't know how to pray. Our best prayer, either as a group or as individuals, is to merely present ourselves as temples for the Spirit to occupy. We don't have to get it right when we pray, we just have to give ourselves to God. That doesn't mean that we can plead ignorance and ineptitude as an excuse for not praying. Prayer is a discipline that we will follow if we truly want to grow. We will make and meet commitments to turn our attention to God as best we can in light of personal aptitudes and other duties. We will keep praying, corporately and individually, even when it seems we are getting nothing out of it, or if it seems we are doing it wrong, because it is not only about us.

Prayer is about everyone: it is about you and me as individuals, it is about God, and it is about every other person who has or will be in this world, whether they pray or not. We are not alone. We are surrounded and sustained by the Spirit of God filling the entire world as well as filling the individual souls of people at prayer around the world now, throughout history, and for ages to come. Some of the prayers sustaining us now might come from nuns, monks, and their guests who in the roughly seventeen hundred years of Christian monasticism have recited psalms that did not match their mood. We should be grateful for that, and one of the best ways to express our gratitude is for us to join in the psalmody.

With Gratitude in our Hearts: A Sermon for St. Benedict's Day

By Abbot Andrew

From the Fall 2000 Abbey Letter

After the rich young man left Jesus, heavy of heart because his possessions were many, the disciples reminded Jesus that they had given up everything to follow him and then asked what they were going to get in exchange for their sacrifice. This question is enough to make one wonder if the disciples thought they were superstars entitled to renegotiate their contracts. They show here a cold-hearted approach to our choices in life, an approach filled with sober calculation as to what we have to gain from doing one thing rather than another. From that sort of attitude, it is a short step to not caring what we do as long as life is reasonably comfortable. In the end, love is frozen out by degrees where we don't see what is happening until it is too late.

In his reply, Jesus promised the disciples that they would sit on twelve thrones judging the twelve tribes of Israel. This sounds pretty glamorous until one thinks about how uncomfortable fancy thrones can be to sit on and how dull courtroom proceedings are when Perry

Mason isn't around. Maybe Jesus was poking fun at the disciples for asking such a silly question. But when Jesus goes on to promise his followers that they will receive what they have given up a hundredfold and eternal life as well, it appears that Jesus understands that it is difficult, if not impossible, for us to sacrifice ourselves without receiving something in return. We may be willing to give up what the IRS calls a tangible benefit as long as we receive the intangible benefit of feeling good, but that is about the limit for many people.

The author of Proverbs, however, offers us an alternative way at looking at this matter:

> *My child, if you accept my words*
> *and treasure up my commandments within you,*
> *making your ear attentive to wisdom*
> *and inclining your heart to understanding;*
> *if you indeed cry out for insight,*
> *and raise your voice for understanding;*
> *if you seek it like silver,*
> *and search for it as for hidden treasures*
> *then you will understand the fear of the Lord*
> *and find the knowledge of God.*

These words, so dear to Benedict's heart, suggest that if we make our ears attentive to wisdom, we will seek for it as if it were a hidden treasure. If we really care about the treasure we are seeking, then we will not calculate the risks and trouble that the search causes us. We will be too interested in the search. Our hearts will be in it. When Jesus says that our heart will be where our treasure is, he is, of course, posing the question: What do we treasure in life? Do we treasure anything at all?

Likewise, the parable of the pearl of great value in Matthew's Gospel jolts us out of our complacency about what we value in life. A merchant who will impulsively sell everything for just one pearl, however valuable, is not showing the best business sense in the world, especially not in these days when diversification is the norm. Surely a merchant who calculates what the pearl is actually worth will conclude

that it is not worth giving up everything for it. We have to hedge our bets better than that. But that is what the merchant does not do. A merchant who gives up everything for the pearl does not count the cost because the full measure of that cost can't be known until it is too late. This merchant is so consumed by desire for the pearl that all business calculations are flung out the window.

Jesus emphasizes the need to treasure God's kingdom beyond all calculation when he speaks of those who, unlike those made eunuchs by birth or human agency, have made themselves eunuchs for the sake of the kingdom of heaven. This verse has traditionally been used as a proof text for the legitimacy of celibacy in Christianity, and Jesus is certainly using the term here in a figurative sense. This verse, however, can help us reflect on the nature of whatever sacrifice is required of us in any vocation. Here, sacrifices are not made grimly in the hope that making ourselves miserable will prove worthwhile some day. Rather, sacrifices are spontaneous responses to something that carries us away. Those who make themselves eunuchs for the kingdom of heaven are not making a rational decision as to what will help them get ahead in life. No, these are people who so deeply treasure the kingdom of heaven that they pay little attention to what they are giving up for the sake of this treasure.

It is possible, though, to see the parables in Luke about the person who tried to build a tower and the king who started a war as suggesting that we do need to count the cost of following Jesus. Or might Jesus be suggesting that the economics of building and the strategy of war are radically different from the kingdom of God? Perhaps the kingdom of God is the sort of menu where, if you need to see the price, you cannot afford it. Quantitative measures don't apply where God is concerned.

Being consumed with enthusiasm for God's kingdom and for what we believe God is calling us to do does not mean that we hop, skip, and jump through all of life's difficulties as if they weren't there. What I mean is that the Holy Spirit gives us enough burning energy to overcome the obstacles and frustrations that come our way. A writer who is consumed by a writing project does not give up when each word comes at the cost of much sweat. Neither does that writer try to figure out if the pain of searching for the right expressions is worth it. A writer who counts the cost isn't deeply involved in writing. A couple that breaks up over their first disagreement have not fallen very deeply in love. A novice who has fallen in love with the monastic life does not leave at the first hint of boredom during the Divine Office.

Falling in love is not, of course, something strictly under our control. A man doesn't make an evaluation of a woman he knows, tally up a balance sheet, and then make up his mind whether or not he loves her. A woman does not make a list of the virtues of chemistry and then decide if she loves chemistry or not. No more did I measure the worth of monasticism and come to the conclusion that it would be a good idea to fall in love with that way of life. It would be just as reasonable to withhold our love from God until we have figured out whether or not God comes up to our standards of a competent deity. No, first we fall in love, and then we fumble for reasons as to why it was a wonderful thing that it happened. If we happen to find any reasons, we usually realize that these reasons would not have been found if love had not spurred us on to search for them.

Although falling in love is something that happens to us, we are not likely to be overpowered by another person, an idea for a story, or the monastic life without going on a treasure hunt. It is possible to stumble over a treasure without looking for it, but looking for it greatly increases the chances we will find it. If we search, we will find; if we knock, the door will be opened for us. We must, then, cultivate within ourselves an openness to finding God's treasure, a willingness to fall in love. In cultivating this openness, we are already throwing calculation to the winds. If, instead, all we are looking for is the best deal, we will find it, but the best deal is not a treasure and it has nothing to do with love.

For me, asking for entry into a monastic community was the result of having fallen in love with the monastic package: the round of worship, the work, the study, shared life with others. This is a love which keeps me going through the times when this way of life does not seem to be the most glamorous or exciting way to live. Like any vocation that takes time to unfold, the monastic life is a treasure that is rediscovered year after year as I stay with it. It isn't a case of giving up a number of things for God for the sake of receiving something in return. It is more of a case that the monastic life is itself the cause of my gratitude to God. From my first years as a monk, I remember being impressed during the intercessions at Mass, when Fr. Anthony, my novice master, offered thanksgiving for his monastic vocation. I was feeling that way myself at the time and, over the years, my monastic vocation continues to be a source of gratitude. It isn't a case of living the monastic life in the hope that I will get a reward from God for my pains. The vocation is itself a reward for what I haven't even done yet. Much of this feeling was caught by St. Paul when he wrote, "With gratitude in your hearts sing psalms, hymns, and spiritual songs to God." That is what I feel that I do when I join the monastic community for worship. Surely God wants all of us, whatever our calling, "to run on the path of God's commandments, our hearts overflowing with the inexpressible delight of love." This is what Benedict promises those who follow the monastic life, and surely that is what God promises to all who seek the kingdom as if searching for hidden treasure.

Part Three:

SPIRITUAL REFLECTIONS

What Kind of God Do We Really Want?
By Br. Martin

From the Summer 2007 Abbey Letter

Over the years the story of Jonah has become one of my favorite stories in the Old Testament. If one reads it carefully, one discovers that it is full of details that provide much food for thought. Ironically, since the story of Jonah is often taught to children in Sunday school, we as adults are often blind to its various levels of meaning. We think we know the story, but do we really?

One of the first ironic details is God telling Jonah to go to Nineveh to preach repentance to its inhabitants. That is, God is telling him to go to the capital of Israel's enemies to warn them to turn from their evil ways, or else. Jonah does not want mercy to be shown to his enemies, so he books passage on a boat on its way to Tarshish, in the opposite direction. Jonah is trying to run from God.

God sends a storm to the ship to stop Jonah's flight. I am fascinated by the portrayal of the sailors. They are not of the same faith as Jonah, yet they recognize that God sent the storm for one reason or another. It is only after exhausting all means of survival that they cast lots to see who is at fault. The lot of course falls to Jonah, who confesses his flight from God. But even then, even after Jonah tells them to throw him overboard to save themselves, they continue to try to survive the storm by rowing through it rather than by sacrificing the guilty one. And in the end, when they do consent to throwing Jonah overboard, they are clearly very reluctant in doing so, praying that they not be guilty of innocent blood.

Within this incident we have the classic structure for scapegoating. There is a crisis (a storm at sea threatening to break up the boat), and so to alleviate the crisis, the one foreigner is singled out to blame (Jonah, a Jew), and is sacrificed (thrown overboard), thus bringing peace. Yet ironically, we see that the sailors are very reluctant to sacrifice anyone, even after Jonah admits the storm is his fault. I cannot help but suspect that they intuitively, perhaps even unconsciously, understand that such behavior does not bring lasting peace. Yet they don't know what else to do.

I believe what does happen is God's answer to their reluctance. He saves Jonah by having him swallowed by a large fish. Early church

theologians saw all kinds of foreshadowing in this particular event. For example, they saw Jonah's being tossed overboard as an image of baptism. Being in the fish for three days and nights symbolized Jesus being dead for three days. Jonah's being spewed onto shore was seen as a foreshadowing of Jesus' resurrection. I do not reject any of this. But I also tend to think that God is hinting at the futility of scapegoating and is providing a way out of it, which is: Don't scapegoat.

After being spewed onto shore, Jonah is once again told by God to go to Nineveh to preach repentance to its inhabitants, which Jonah, after all he's been through, understandably does. Amazingly, and to Jonah's disappointment, the people of Nineveh do repent, and God spares the city.

Well now, this is too much for Jonah to accept. Being only human, he wants revenge, not redemption, for his enemies. So he spitefully leaves in a huff and angrily says to God: "O Lord! Is not this what I said while I was still in my own country? That is why I fled to Tarshish at the beginning; for I know that you are a gracious God, and merciful, slow to anger, and abounding in steadfast love, and ready to relent from punishing. O Lord, please take my life, for it is better for me to die than to live." God then asks, "Is it right for you to be angry?" With that, Jonah leaves the city to sulk.

God, having all the attributes ascribed to him by Jonah, therefore causes a bush to grow to give shade to Jonah, who is grateful. The next day, God causes the bush to whither and die. I wonder if this ironic detail is in the story partly in order for God to mildly inflict on Jonah the punishment Jonah wants God to inflict on Nineveh. Anyway, Jonah is not ready to give up his anger and resentment, his desire to have the inhabitants of Nineveh ruthlessly destroyed. God asks, "Is it right for you to be angry about the bush?" Jonah answers, "Yes, angry enough to die"!

I am struck by God's gentle reply: "You are concerned about a bush, for which you did not labor and which you did not cause to grow...And should I not be concerned about Nineveh, that great city, in which are more than a hundred twenty-thousand persons...and also many animals?"

Again, it is important to understand that God is talking about his loving concern for an enemy of his chosen people. The irony is that God cares as much for those whom we demonize, call evil, or name as our enemy, as we believe he cares for us. Do we really want a God of just, yet merciless, retribution, or do we want the God revealed over the ages as loving all of us, friend and foe alike? Are we, like Jonah, not ready for the latter?

Brando, Cher, & Me

By Fr. William

From the Easter 2005 Abbey Letter

What's your favorite confession scene in the movies? I don't mean a criminal confessing to the authorities, but a scene with a Christian making a sacramental confession to a priest. I have two. There's one from *The Appaloosa*, a Western I saw as a teenager, where the cowboy, played by Marlon Brando, confessed, "I've killed a lot of men and sinned a lot of women. But the men I killed needed killin' and the women wanted sinnin', and well, I never was one much to argue." The other one is in the 1987 comedy, *Moonstruck*, where Cher tries to render a particularly embarrassing sin unobtrusive by slipping it in between taking the Lord's name in vain and bouncing a check at the liquor store. Her ploy fails. Her sin obtrudes.

Movie confessions and real-life confessions are sometimes alike and sometimes different. I doubt many priests ever hear quite the same words the cowboy's priest heard. And I suspect that a lot of people have tried to do what Cher tried to do. So now you may be thinking, Well now I know two things you're not supposed to do in confession. So what is it you are supposed to do?

That's where I come in. I want to use this article to provide some useful information on confession for people whose image of confession is largely formed by what they've seen in the movies and what they may have experienced in therapy or the sharing in support groups.

Although I do hear confessions as part of my ministry at the Abbey, my main claim to expertise in this area is that I'm a big, fat sinner, and have been going to confession for nearly forty years now.

My main reason for wanting to address this particular topic at this time of year is that these final days of Lent are a perfect time for people to make use of the ministry the Prayer Book calls The Reconciliation of a Penitent. Lent is a time to recognize and confess our sins, and return to a life of grace, and what better way could there be for doing that than explicitly recognizing and confessing our sins, and returning to a life of grace?

When we come to confession, we're having one of those "I'm sorry, please take me back" conversations with our beloved. In those conversations, we admit that what we said, did, or thought was wrong, really wrong; we say that we are sorry; and we pledge that we are going to work not to do those things again. Our beloved's—our Lord's—part in this conversation is spoken by the priest who hears our confession. That sort of conversation may be difficult, but when we've gone astray, it's healthy and healing. Sometimes it's even necessary, if we're going to keep the relationship alive. So for what it's worth, here's an old hand's suggestions on how to go about having that particular conversation with Jesus.

Getting Ready

If you're new to sacramental confession, read Pages 446- 452 of the Book of Common Prayer and also the Q&A on the Reconciliation of a Penitent on Page 861.

Some Episcopal churches have regularly scheduled times for confession, but in most parishes, you will have to make an appointment. That will mean setting the time and place for your confession, as with any appointment. You will also want to decide the format of the confession, that is: will you use Form One or Form Two, or a face to face conversation leading to absolution? Some people like to combine one of the Prayer Book rites with the less formal conversational style.

If this is your first sacramental confession, let the priest know that.

First confessions tend to be longer than the subsequent ones. And the priest will probably want to ask if you want some help in preparing for your confession.

That preparation will consist of prayer and self-examination. If this is your first confession, you need to examine your moral life since your Baptism. If you've used the sacrament of confession before, review the period since your last confession. If the period under review is a long one, you will find yourself looking mostly at trends and habits. But it's also important to note the individual acts of serious sin as well. If your last confession was relatively recent, then the focus tends to be more on individual sinful acts.

In your self-examination, it's good to consult both your own conscience and some reliable outside source as well. The Ten Commandments, expounded in the Prayer Book Catechism, give a directly Biblical source for this. The traditional lists of the seven deadly sins or of the seven cardinal and theological virtues give a more analytical approach to the demands of Christian morality. Most of the lists for self-examination you find in devotional manuals are based on one of these three sources. There is also a list of eight moral shortcomings taken from Cassian's *Institutes* that is widely used in monastic circles. Maybe our Novice Master will write an article on that someday.

Some authorities advise making notes during your examination of conscience to use in making your confession. Others discourage this, because reading from a list makes the act of confession itself somewhat mechanical, and because there are dangers in putting embarrassing things down in writing. My own observation is that for confessions covering a short period, going by memory works fine. But after putting in the time and effort to review a larger piece of my life, I wouldn't want the frustration of leaving the church after the rite was all finished and done with, and then thinking of something I'd meant to confess, but had forgotten during the confession itself. So I think notes are a good idea for that sort of confession.

Get to church early enough to spend a little time in prayer and recollection before you actually begin your confession. If you're having a conference-type confession in the priest's office, spend a bit of time in prayer before you arrive for your appointment.

Making Your Confession

You don't need to go into a great deal of detail about your sins. But the confessor does need to know what you're talking about. Usually you can follow the guideline that you confess what you did wrong, but not how you went about doing it.

If you are aware of the reasons for your sins, that you did something out of jealousy or pride for instance, it's good to say that as part of your confession. But don't get lost in examining your motivations. Remember this is confession, not therapy. If something would be off topic or too self-centered in an "I'm sorry, please take me back" conversation with your beloved, it would probably be off-topic in confession.

Make sure you confess your own sins, and don't slide into reporting on what other people have done wrong. In fact, it's considered better form not to refer to others in ways that reveal their identities. Still, you will probably have to mention other people from time to time in reference to your relationship to them for your confession to be accurate. "I have been disrespectful towards and dismissive of one particular person's ideals," and "I have been disrespectful towards and dismissive of my wife's ideals," are somewhat different statements.

Your confessor will probably give you a penance to do (this is the assignment described in the next to last paragraph on Page 446 of the Prayer Book). It's best to take care of this right away, if at all possible. That's not because your absolution depends on it. It doesn't. But if you don't do it promptly, you might forget about it. And when you finally remember it, you'll feel bad, and you'll miss some of the benefits of going through every element of the rite.

Speaking of forgetting: if you do forget to mention something in your confession that you meant to, don't worry about it too much. Absolution is the restoration of a good relationship with God, and covers the sins you have forgotten. If you want to say in your next confession, "I meant to say this in my last confession, but forgot to. I know it's forgiven, but I'd like to confess it anyway," that would be fine. If the forgotten sin was a serious one, you really should mention it in this way. But your earlier confession and its absolution are valid and sacramentally complete even if you don't.

Finally, when your confession is over, and you've received your absolution and performed your penance, spend a little bit of time in prayer. Say the things you say after one of those, "I'm sorry, please take me back" conversations. Tell the Lord, "Thank you for taking me back." And say, "I love you, really love you." But you already knew that part, didn't you?

On Being Spiritual and Religious
By Abbot Andrew

From the Summer 2008 Abbey Letter

"I'm spiritual, but not religious," is a refrain we hear often these days. As with most popular expressions, its meaning is vague, but it's quite clear that the expression makes a distinction between being spiritual and being religious with the implication that they are alternatives. A brief reflection on what the distinction seems to mean should give us some insight into a prevalent attitude floating in the air.

I take the expression spiritual but not religious to indicate an interest in supernatural reality of some sort lived out with consciousness-raising practices such as meditation, but separate from any particular religious institution. There might be respect for some teachings in some religions, but these teachings are brought together in a personal eclectic mix. This approach to being spiritual isn't new. Ralph Waldo Emerson and Henry David Thoreau did much to sell Americans and people world-wide on a spirituality of self-reliance.

It is telling that I can't recall ever hearing anybody turn the expression around by claiming to be religious, but not spiritual. This suggests that religious people don't see anything wrong with being spiritual, and are not likely to see the two as alternatives. Apparently, spiritual people see religion as an obstacle to spirituality, but religious people don't see spirituality as an obstacle to religion.

The Latin root word for religion, *religare*, means to bind. Religious practices live up to this meaning by making connections that bind people with each other and with God. Practices of spirituality are also capable of making these connections, but if spirituality is separated from religion, then whatever good they do for an individual's well-being, any connections they make with other human beings or God are tenuous at best. Basically, a person who is spiritual but not religious follows the spiritual quest alone. The extreme of this would be to live by Plotinus' famous phrase: The alone to the Alone.

A condescending attitude comes across to me in the claim to be spiritual but not religious. It seems to suggest that religion is beneath one who is really spiritual. I'm sure that is not always the case with everybody who says this, but when I look back on my years of adolescence and early adulthood, I have to admit frankly that this sort of snobbishness was a large ingredient in my own outlook that fit the phrase spiritual but not religious forty years before it became common currency. Maybe my perception at the time that religious people usually weren't all that spiritual was true. I do see a lot more vital interest in spirituality in churches today than I remember seeing then, but there

is also a real possibility that my snobbish attitude made it harder for me to see the spirituality that really was present in religious people.

In all fairness to people who are inclined to be spiritual but not religious, it must be admitted that, in religion, we do not always connect to the right things in the right way. The French thinker René Girard has done much to draw our attention to how, traditionally, societies have pulled themselves together by perpetuating collective violence via a scapegoating mechanism. Some religions have bound their people together in precisely this way. It's understandable that sensitive people would shy away from any religious group that binds itself together by defining common enemies and outcasts. It can easily seem preferable to forge one's own path, however lonely it is, than to connect with a group that disconnects from other people in violent ways.

A decisive factor that led to my becoming religious as well as spiritual was a growing dissatisfaction with the eclectic approach. I reached a point where I realized that, in order for my spirituality to be centered, it had to be rooted in a particular religious tradition. My settling on Christianity, however, was not made with the sense that one choice was as good as another. At the time of my decision, Christ, who very definitely willed certain things, such as fellowship with me, became very real to me. God's grace and my choice to give myself to the particular Personhood of Christ were so inextricably entwined that there is no way I can separate one from the other. Particular is the key word here. The missing ingredient in spirituality without religion is particularity. Before this conversion, it seemed that believing in an impersonal god, whose manifestation on earth was not limited to one holy person, preserved my individuality. The irony is, that it is the making of particular choices in terms of friends, a community, and God that has enhanced my own particular individuality.

One of the particularities of Christianity is that the Holy Spirit makes spirituality religious by binding people and God together. The Holy Spirit is more than the bond of love between the Father and the Son. The Holy Spirit is a Person who actively brings the Father and the Son together and also actively brings each one of us, in our own particularity, to the Father and the Son and to each other in that same bond of Love. That Holy Spirit inspires us to love everybody, not in general, but in particular. This does not mean that the Holy Spirit gives us the impossible task of relating personally with billions of people. Rather, the Holy Spirit inspires us to follow Jesus' commandment to love our neighbors. Our neighbors are the particular people who happen to be present in our lives. With the Holy Spirit binding us together with God in this way, there is no room for binding together by way of collective violence. This is how the Holy Spirit makes religion spiritual.

Living spiritually and religiously requires that we face the challenge of living with our own particularity and the particularity of others. We cannot meet this challenge without commitment: commitment to God and commitment to our neighbors. It is easy to be tempted to shrink from this challenge. I had something of a relapse into being more spiritual than religious when I first considered a monastic vocation. I thought I could relate to God and grow spiritually with little reference to the other members of the community if they weren't holy enough to my liking. But I learned very quickly that only by committing myself to

the particular monks in this place could I grow spiritually. This is why Benedict puts so much emphasis on commitment in his Rule. Benedict has only disapproval for wandering monastics who hop from place to place without ever settling down. Such people are committed neither to God nor to other people. The Benedictine vow of stability of place is precisely a vow of commitment to God *and* to the particular people in a particular place, and the land and the trees, to say nothing of the cats. This kind of commitment may not sound as spiritual as attaining cosmic consciousness, but it is by living with particular people who give us daily opportunities to make little sacrifices that we receive clear indications of when we are living in the Bond of Love of the Holy Spirit and when we are not.

Far from being a restrictive god who imposes a tyrannical rule on us, the God who calls us to commitment models total commitment to us, a commitment that took Jesus to the cross. The Persons of the Holy Trinity are totally committed to each other as much as they are totally committed to each one of us. We might be too busy to attend to a family member, a friend, or a community member, but the Holy Spirit has all the time in the world, plus Eternity, to be the Bond of Love between each of us and the Father and the Son. The Holy Spirit fills the whole world by virtue of this full-time commitment. What that means to us is that the Holy Spirit is intimately involved in the smallest details of our commitments to our neighbors and God. As the flame who formed tongues of fire above the disciples, the Holy Spirit breathes life into our smallest acts of service to each other and in the prayers we offer together to God. Serving others at table and vacuuming hallways may not be the sorts of things that make newspaper headlines, but, in the Holy Spirit, they are of cosmic importance.

It is true that I made a caricature of people who are spiritual but not religious at the beginning of this article. I know that many such people honestly struggle to participate in connections that the Holy Spirit is forging. Likewise, the notion that religious people are not spiritual is a caricature that blinds one to many of the ways the Holy Spirit breathes life into corporate activities. Both caricatures are harmful when they are used to denigrate other people. These caricatures are of some use, however, if they are turned toward ourselves and used as monitors for religious and spiritual growth. Is there real binding in our spirituality? Does the fire of the Holy Spirit breathe through our prayer and our acts of service to others? When the answer to both questions is Yes, our hearts are inflamed as we walk with Jesus as did the disciples on the Road to Emmaus.

Blast from the Past
By Br. Abraham

From the Fall 2005 Abbey Letter

Stories from the past are important to society. They remind us of former struggles, gains, and losses so that we can learn from them and try to avoid earlier mistakes while at the same time building on the good foundations laid by our ancestors. The stories told in monasteries serve the same function, and are an important part of monastic education and formation. Most frequently, these are heard in informal settings such as the times before meals when those monks assigned for the week are putting food on the plates to be served to the other monks and guests, or at times of recreation when the community gathers in the common room for conversation. One story that I heard as a novice has stuck with me ever since, and has greatly influenced my understanding of love. The story involved two junior monks (those between their years of novitiate and profession of life vows), one of whom told the other, "If this were truly a Christian place, people wouldn't do things that upset me." The one who said it didn't stay in the monastery very long. He was confused about love.

We all suffer from the same confusion at times. We mistakenly think that others who profess to love God and follow Jesus will do so only in ways that we understand and approve. We wrongly expect people to show their love for God and neighbor by behaving only in ways with which we are comfortable and that buttress our own beliefs, rather than causing us to question our assumptions. The life of Jesus teaches us how wrong we are. Jesus upset almost everyone at some point, and yet he loved them all. His example teaches us how to truly love by seeing people as they are and accepting them as they are, while expecting them to grow, hoping and praying for their growth, and joyfully respecting their ultimate maturity as images of God—all unique, beautiful images different from each other but still images of the infinite God.

Many times we think we love someone or feel loved while in a certain group, but are actually merely enjoying the emotional high that the person or group brings us. Once again, Jesus showed us that this is not true love, because he loved even those who hated him and made life miserable for him. To love someone truly, we must love the person, not just the way the person makes us feel. True love is based not on subjectivity, but on the objective desire that everyone reach their full potential, no matter how different it is from our own. Adopting that understanding of love does not excuse wrong behavior, but it does involve being concerned with the difficult task of correcting such behavior and preventing it in the future. Healing the victims and perpetrators of wrongdoings is more important than the easier and quicker option of punishing people out of anger or righteous indignation. Punishing people might make us feel better, but it rarely solves problems, and love is much more concerned with solving problems than with feeling good. Love consists in expanding our hearts in order to give everyone a place there, no matter how uncomfortable it may be to invite some people in.

The expansion of our hearts in love is important, because we must avoid the opposite habit of gripping things tightly to our chests out of fear. We must never confuse love with control. Love wants the best for people, but realizes that what is best for them is not necessarily the same as what is safest and most comfortable for us. Love is supportive of the other person's path, and allows that person to travel it, even though it would seem easier if every one were on the same road. (We do have the right and the obligation to intervene carefully in lives that are self-destructive or that hurt others.) There is a good story about these different paths from Dorotheus of Gaza, a seventh century monk from Palestine:

> *Imagine a circle marked on the ground. Suppose that the circle is the world and that the center of the circle is God. Leading from the edge to the center are a number of lines, representing ways of life. In their desire to draw near to God, the saints advance along the lines to the middle of the circle, so that the further they go, the nearer they approach to one another as well as to God. The closer they come to God, the closer they come to one another. Such is the nature of love: the nearer we draw to God in love, the more we are united together by love for our neighbor.*

Love allows our neighbors to follow their paths; fear tries to control the paths that others follow so that we are never confronted by the discomforting possibility that we ourselves might be heading the wrong way. Love holds everything and everyone dearly in our hearts, always expanding so that others can grow in their unique vocations. Fear grips others tightly to our chests so that they don't have a chance to be different from us.

One way we can stop fearing and start loving is by heeding Jesus' advice to not worry about the speck in our neighbor's eye, and instead to deal with the log in our own eye. We often use the log as both a telescope and a club—a telescope to magnify the speck in our neighbor's eye, and a club to beat that neighbor over the head. The only way to come to terms with the log in our eye is to admit to ourselves and to God that it is there. Then it becomes much easier to live with and to work to heal it. We might find that the log in our eye is something that is truly harmful and needs to be corrected, but until we admit that it is there, nothing can be done about it. Then again, it might simply be part of our personality that we were embarrassed by but which we can now come to see as part of our unique being to be embraced and allowed to flourish. But as long as we keep gripping it to beat others with, or polishing it to magnify the specks in other's eyes, we can't really love, because having a log in our eye blocks and skews our vision, and love is not blind. Love sees all quite clearly and still loves. Love loves the person, not just the way the person makes us feel. By coming to terms with the log in our eye, we can then truly begin to love ourselves and follow the command of Jesus to love God and our neighbors as ourselves. But until we love ourselves, we can not love our neighbors as ourselves, and we can't love the God who made us the way we are.

People may upset us from time to time, and while it may be true that they do need to change their actions, we must also be ready to accept the fact that perhaps their ways are exactly as they are meant to be. In those cases, we should be happy for them and grateful for their existence as individuals growing into their vocations as children of God. Doing that frees us from the crushing burden and smothering bondage of judging and controlling others so that we can instead joyfully take on the easy yoke and light burden of Jesus as we follow him in our own unique way. Jesus' yoke of freedom unites us all to himself so that we do not need to worry about the way that others are united to him, as Dorotheus of Gaza reminds us. We are then free to hold the world in our hearts in love. We are then free to truly love people, instead of hoping that they will make us feel good and manipulating them in order to prolong the feeling. We are then free to see everything about each person and love them anyway, because we know that God knows us more than anyone else ever could and yet loves us more than anyone else ever could. We are then free to differ with individuals and groups while still affirming their integrity, so that we can avoid saying embarrassing things like: "If this were truly a Christian place, people wouldn't do things that upset me."

St. Gregory's Abbey is truly a Christian place, but sometimes people here do things that upset me (the vast majority of the time, the source of the distress is my own skewed vision caused by the many logs in my eyes). More often, I do things that upset others here. Fortunately, the other monks are much more securely grounded in love than I am, so they forgive my wrongdoings and forbear my idiosyncrasies, while still expecting me to mature in my actions and attitudes. I only hope that my own struggles learning to love may someday be of help to others, as the story I heard as a novice in the common room about the upset junior monk from years past has helped me. I am grateful to him, wherever he is and whatever he is doing. May we grow together as we grow toward God.

Homily for Trinity Sunday
By Fr. Aelred

From the Fall 1999 Abbey Letter

Since the publication of Jürgen Moltmann's *The Trinity and the Kingdom of God* in 1981, more and more books about the Holy Trinity have appeared. We get a lot of them and I read most of them. It seems to me that books about the Holy Trinity are almost never mediocre but either extraordinarily bad and boring or astonishingly intriguing and exciting.

One that I found to be in the latter category is *These Three are One: The Practice of Trinitarian Theology* by David S. Cunningham. Some will find his avoidance of the term person and his attempts to find alternative names for the Father, Son, and Holy Spirit aggravating, but he explains his reasoning. And I think that an author who is courteous enough to take the trouble to apologize for making a daring attempt to accomplish something worthwhile deserves a sympathetic hearing.

Cunningham says that one extremely important aspect of Moltmann's book and the works that have been inspired by it is the insistence that belief in the Trinity ought to make a difference. What one truly believes ought to manifest itself in how one acts. The Trinity ought not to be an optional extra. Nor should it be seen as a matter of earning merit in a religious game, as if one were increasingly holy the more numerous the incomprehensible things one affirmed. This is all well and good, but the problem, according to Cunningham, is that the statements about what belief in the Holy Trinity ought to mean in terms of how we live our lives are so vague and bland that they don't really say anything at all—certainly nothing that is connected with belief in the Holy Trinity. Cunningham examines what the consequences of a truly Trinitarian outlook ought to be in various topics, including sex and violence in a way that would appall Pat Robertson, but I was gratified that any author would suggest concrete ways in which belief in the Trinity should make a difference in how you live your life. That is what is important—how you live your life.

But I don't intend to go into that—there is no time to follow all his reasoning in a sermon. Read the book. Instead, I want to look at how he approaches the mystery of the Trinity itself. He notes something that I have commented on earlier—that writers about the Holy Trinity either begin with God and then try to show that God is three persons or begin with the three persons and then try to show that they are one God. Logically one might think that one has to begin someplace—at one end or the other of the loaf, as one might say, but Cunningham suggests that this is only because we are asking the question incorrectly.

He begins neither with the one and the many nor with the many and the one, but with relationships. It was all interesting and pretty abstract and was just added to my porous memory without making a great impression, but the seed was planted.

The catalyst was another book, this one not about the Holy Trinity (though, to take Cunningham's suggestion to a logical conclusion, if the book is about something true, it ought to manifest, however vestigially, the truth of the Trinity). The book was The *Puppet of Desire: The Psychology of Hysteria, Possession, and Hypnosis* by Jean-Michel Oughourlian. I don't normally go in for that sort of topic, but Oughourlian is an interpreter of the theories of René Girard, so I looked at his book.

He said that one of the great post-Enlightenment myths about personality is that there is a real self. He said that the self as it differs in all its relationships is all the real self—that relationships make the self. He was saying the same sort of thing that Cunningham was saying about God, but he was saying it about me. It was no abstraction any longer but as real as myself. There is a post-Cartesian myth that we are autonomous individuals who freely to choose to enter into relationships. It is not true. I am the product of relationships—those between my parents, between my parents and myself, relationships that everyone and every group I have ever encountered has had with me and with every other entity that has ever been in relationship with any other. Existence is relationships.

If God exists, then God is in relationship. If God is the creator, as Judaism, Christianity and Islam teach, then he must have been in relationship with himself before creation. Rather than the Trinity's being an unnecessary abstraction, it is a necessary truth. If existence is relationships, then a God who is not a Trinity could not exist. Because He does, we do.

Working for the Kingdom
By Br. Cuthbert

From the Fall 2009 Abbey Letter

I wish I could say that I *get* the parable of the landowner who goes out at different times during the day to hire laborers to work in his vineyard (Matthew 20: 1-16). I wish I could say that I connect with it, that I appreciate its meaning, and that I fully agree with the point that Jesus is making about the kingdom of heaven. But if I'm honest here, then I have to admit that I have some problems with it. For one, my sense of economic fairness makes me a little uncomfortable with the idea of handing out a full day's pay for only an hour's worth of work. It's not that I identify with the workers who were hired early in the morning, or those who were hired late in the afternoon, for that matter. From as objective a viewpoint as I am able to have, it's merely a sense of economic principle that makes me question the wisdom of paying everyone the same thing. I know that God's foolishness is wiser than human wisdom, and that human wisdom is foolishness to God, but on the surface, it just seems a bit odd. And since I'm not theologically astute enough to delve into the whole faith vs. works argument, I just try to meet the parable on its own terms with the capacity I have to understand it, and it sounds kind of unfair.

To look at it another way, elsewhere in the gospels, Jesus talks about how hard it is to enter the kingdom of heaven: "Strive to enter by the narrow gate for the gate is narrow and the road is hard that leads to life," and "those who wish to be my disciples must take up their cross daily and follow me," and, "those who put a hand to the plow and look back are not fit for the kingdom of heaven," and, "those who persevere to the end will be saved." From this, it sounds like one has to put forth a real effort if one wants the reward of being admitted to the kingdom of heaven. It sounds like it is not that easy to get there. And this only makes sense from a work-ethic point of view which holds that through hard work and perseverance one will succeed in reaching one's goal—a work ethic I think most people would agree with.

But in the gospel parable, Jesus is saying that even if you put forth a real effort, work as hard as you can to enter the kingdom of heaven and end up getting there, then you might be in the company of those who did not work nearly as much and yet who are enjoying the same reward that you had to strive so hard to attain. And while it would be nice to have a magnanimous attitude of, Oh, it's just great that everyone gets to come in no matter what they have or haven't done, it still just seems unbalanced to me that this great reward for which so many have struggled and suffered—some even to the point of dying for it—should also be given equally to those who did little or almost nothing to attain it.

And it's not that I think that those who work harder deserve more than what they set out to achieve. But surely those who *don't* work

as hard don't *deserve* the same amount that is given to the diligent, right?

Of course, Jesus does make the point in the parable that when it comes to the kingdom of God, it is God's to give it to whomever he wishes to give it, and it's not ours to question it, and that's fair enough. The Lord does whatever he wills, but still I can understand the annoyance of the workers who were hired early in the morning and had to bear the heat of the day and who then see a group of latecomers who do a minimal amount of work receive the same payment.

Is there, then, anything to suggest that those who work harder to attain the kingdom of God receive a greater reward, or that those who don't work very hard to attain the kingdom of God receive a lesser reward? Is there anything that might make this situation seem just a bit more economically fair?

At the outset, I will say that I don't think the kingdom of God has any degrees. If you're in, you're in, and it's the same blessedness, the same joy, the same love that is shared by all who are there. So I don't think that the ultimate reward—the usual daily wage of Jesus' parable—can be either increased or decreased; regardless of what effort one puts into getting there. But I do think that there is an additional reward for those who work harder to get there, and the reward is the work itself.

Consider what kind of work one has to do to attain the kingdom of God. *The Rule of St. Benedict* has a list of such good works, among which are: "to love the Lord God with the whole heart, the whole soul, the whole strength, to love one's neighbor as oneself, to relieve the poor, to visit the sick, to help in trouble, not to give way to anger, not to nurse a grudge, to put one's hope in God, to hate no one, not to be jealous, not to harbor envy, to pray for one's enemies in the love of Christ, and never despair of God's mercy." It seems that the work one must undertake to attain the kingdom of God, while not always easy, surely would make the worker a happier individual because they would know that the work they are doing is making the kingdom of God not something to be had at some point in the future as a reward for a job done, but as a reality right here, right now in the midst of the work that is going on. Those who are standing idle in the marketplace are doing just that—standing idle, so they are missing out on the reward of the work that is being done.

So, yes, the ultimate reward for everyone who works for the kingdom of God is the kingdom of God; it's salvation; it's that we get to be with Jesus. And I don't think that is a prize that can be increased or diminished. But for those who are working hard to win that prize while others stand idle, it seems to me that the work itself is their bonus pay.

Baptizing the Imagination
By Abbot Andrew

From the Summer 2011 Abbey Letter

In *Surprised by Joy*, C.S. Lewis describes his chance encounter with a book he found in a book stall at a train station that played an important role in his conversion to Christianity. Its title was *Phantastes* and its author, George MacDonald. With hindsight, Lewis realized that, through the novel's enchanted landscape, his "imagination was, in a certain sense, baptized." Here, Lewis uses the term baptized in a sub-Christian sense to show how the vision of George MacDonald led him to Christianity. At the time he first read the book, he was overwhelmed, drenched, by the enchantment of MacDonald's writing. Only later was Lewis overwhelmed by the grace of his baptism when he returned to the faith of his youth, at which time he also appreciated how deeply MacDonald was inspired by the Gospel

In *Phantastes*, Lewis saw "the common things drawn into the bright shadow of the novel's landscape." The same can be said of any good fantasy story. It is impossible to see trees the same way after meeting the Ents in Tolkien's *Lord of the Rings*. Every fresh snowfall is more enchanting after having read of Will Stanton's first journey through a time warp to a wintry landscape in Susan Cooper's *The Dark is Rising*. The unicorn in Madeleine L'Engle's *The Swiftly Tilting*

Planet is so luminous that it casts a spell on everything ever after. (Isn't that what unicorns are for?)

Much of the enchantment of fantasy stories is that they draw us into a world different from the world we normally live in. Usually, imaginary worlds are populated by elves and dwarves, dragons and unicorns. One common way a fantasy world differs from our normal world is through the presence of magic. In the wizard world of the Harry Potter books, magic is so pervasive that it constitutes that world's technology. Mrs. Weasley uses magic to cook dinner as routinely that we muggles turn on an electric stove. Some detractors of these books have complained about the magic in Potter's wizard world, but the presence of magic and its power offers an analogy to the scientific and technological power in our world. Just as magic is a power available for villainous misuse by the likes of Voldemort, so science and technology have the same potential if its users are not morally and spiritually grounded. What C.S. Lewis said about reading *Phantastes* applies to the Potter books: "There was no temptation confuse the scenes of the tale with the light that rested upon them or to suppose that they were put forward as realities." In a magnificent set of novels about a magically gifted boy, Charlie Bone, by Jenny Nimmo, the gifts are fanciful and unique and so are less easily confused with occultism. Charlie's gift,

for example, is the ability to move in and out of pictures such as photographs and paintings, a gift that becomes highly significant in the course of the series.

An imaginary world must show us what kind of world it is, and in so doing, it makes us ask ourselves what kind of universe *we* live in. Lewis' imagination was baptized by MacDonald's novel because, in the end, he saw in Fairyland a reflection of what is true about our world. It is possible, of course, that some fantasy stories might not baptize the imagination in the same way as MacDonald's did. In a way, fantasy worlds are thought experiments that allow us to try other worlds on for size to see what rings good and true about our world.

In defining its world, a fantasy story inevitably puts evil in a cosmic setting. In Susan Cooper's overtly pagan *The Dark is Rising* sequence, the Lords of Light and Lords of Darkness battle each other on roughly equal terms in a dualistic world. On his eleventh birthday, Will Stanton discovers that he is an Old One who must choose which side he will align himself with. The grim Old Ones help humans in peril from the Dark Lords, but they aren't all that friendly, and the power of evil remains an abiding menace that no force can overcome. On the other hand, in *The Lord of the Rings* J.R.R. Tolkien illustrates the Catholic teaching that evil is a lack of substance more profoundly than any theology book possibly could. The Ringwraiths, not to speak of Sauron himself, have lost all substance. There is nothing underneath the ringwraiths' capes, yet they are truly horrifying in their nothingness. The traitor Saruman caps a life gone to moral ruin by melting before Frodo's eyes. Likewise, Voldemort, in the Harry Potter books, has reduced himself to a barely existing malevolent force through dividing his soul into seven items called horcruxes. Regaining his body at the end of the fourth book doesn't give him any more substance than he had before. But the problems in the wizard world cannot all be blamed on Voldemort. Those who oppose this dark lord are undermined by political and social corruptions. The enslavement of elves by good and bad people alike is only one serious symptom. The bad treatment that Harry's godfather, Sirius Black, inflicts on his family's enslaved house elf, Kreacher, has bad consequences for Harry and his friends. In *Phantastes*, Anodos releases a shadow that haunts him for the rest of the story when he opens a door a wise woman told him to leave shut. To combat the evils in Fairyland, Anodos must overcome this darkness that he himself is responsible for.

Goodness is also placed in a cosmic dimension, primarily through magical helpers such as fairy godmothers or talking animals. Such tales suggest that we live in a friendly universe where grace from a higher source is available. The Firebird, for example, gives Prince Ivan a feather that allows him to call her in time of need. In the Charlie Bone books, three uncanny reddish cats known as the Three Flames come to the aid of Charlie and his friends when needed. The fiery imagery of the cats tempts a Christian reader to think of the Holy Spirit. The comical angels, Mrs Whatsit, Mrs Who, and Mrs Which help Meg and Charles Wallace rescue their father from a totalitarian planet and then help Meg rescue her brother when he is captured there. In *The Swiftly*

Tilting Planet, a time unicorn guides Charles Wallace in his rescue mission through time to avert a nuclear war. Aslan's ventures into Narnia are particularly overt illustrations of Divine Providence. *The Lord of the Rings* suggest Divine Providence through the ministry of the magician Gandalf, but more important to this epic is the providential shape of the story as a whole. It is not Frodo who successfully fulfills the anti-quest of destroying the Ring of Power; it is Divine Providence using the loathsome Gollum accomplishes it.

Contrary to these stories, Philip Pullman's series *His Dark Materials* shows a world empty of transcendent helpers. What supernatural creatures there are prove to be malevolent for the most part. Pullman so empties his world of Christ that there is no indication that Jesus or his teaching ever happened in any world. Rick Riordan's set *Percy and the Olympians* brings back to life the Greek and Roman gods where divine providence takes the form of strife between deities who either care little for humans or positively wish to destroy them. Many horror stories suggest that the most powerful beings in the universe are demonic.

Acts of transcendent aid are closely intertwined with moral issues. The Firebird gives Prince Ivan a feather because he took pity on her and freed her instead of keeping her as a hunting trophy. The Flames don't help just anybody, but only those who are aligned with the good intentions of the Red King, the distant ancestor of the magically gifted people in the books. The aid Meg Murray receives from her angelic helpers would not have been enough to rescue Charles Wallace if she had not loved her brother so deeply. A phoenix comes to Harry Potter's aid because of his love for Dumbledore. More importantly, the grace that delivered Harry after his act of sacrifice at the end of the series would have availed nothing if he had not saved the life of his enemy Draco Malfoy not just once, but twice. Likewise, the fulfillment of Frodo's quest depended on his sparing Gollum against Sam's better (but worse) judgment. Contrary to the other stories just mentioned, the heroic journey Will and Lyra make to the land of the dead where everybody is tormented to rescue a friend has no support from a friendly universe. Rather, these two children have to work against the grain of a mostly hostile world. Likewise, the revived Greek and Roman deities offer Percy and his friends no real moral compass, leaving them with only their own fidelity to each other

In *Phantastes,* Anodos is killed when he unveils a demonic religious cult, but then is lifted out of Fairyland and restored to his home where he is alive with a much deeper perspective on life than he had before. Harry Potter and Aslan also die, or seem to, and then continue to live on a higher plane. These and many other stories that follow the outline of the Paschal Mystery baptize the imagination by imagining the world as ultimately redemptive through self-sacrifice in love. However, it is the Gospel which has baptized the human imagination so as to make these stories conceivable. Lewis said his imagination was baptized by MacDonald's novel, but MacDonald's imagination was baptized by the Gospel. It is the imagination baptized by the Gospel that opens our eyes to the shape of the Paschal Mystery in the last Harry Potter book and even in the graceless world of *His Dark Materials.* Will and Lyra's rescue mission to the land of the dead is most likely modeled on Orpheus' attempted rescue of Eurydice, but this venture also has the shape of Christ's harrowing of Hell. It seems that even the imaginations of some atheists are baptized by the Gospel. Death and resurrection is a common scenario in myth, but the Gospel claims to be what Lewis called many times: Myth become fact.

Anodos, Harry Potter and Aslan, in their acts of self-sacrifice, are themselves rescued by a power deeper in the universe than the evil that tried to kill them. Rowling leaves this deeper power rather vague but it is strong enough to bring Harry's dead parents as well as Dumbledore to him as living beings who advise and encourage him in the final steps to defeating Voldemort. When Aslan appears more alive than ever after his death, he points to a deeper writing in the altar on which he was killed, a writing the witch queen could not read. When musing on his renewed life, Anodos recalls a wise woman who assured him that she knew something too good to be told. The baptized imagination discerns this deeper goodness underlying all worlds, a great good that is ever coming, something too good to be told.

Evolution, Creation & God's Love

By Br. Martin

From the Easter 2000 Abbey Letter

It fascinates me that as the new millennium (beginning January 1, 2001) approaches, Darwinian evolutionary theory has once again become controversial, particularly among some Christians. This situation is somewhat understandable, since in some of the more popular presentations of evolution, a number of scientists assert that the theory provides an adequate explanation of the origins of life without recourse to a mythological deity.

While I accept evolution as the best scientific explanation of not only the origins of life and the universe, but also their continual development, I do not accept such a materialistic interpretation. What interests me is what evolution means theologically. If Darwinian evolutionary theory is true, what does that tell us about God and the world we live in?

For one thing, it shows us that creation is not a finished product, but rather that it is an ongoing process. The universe is still expanding, and we are still developing. With Teilhard de Chardin, I believe that there is a directionality to evolution, a goal it is growing towards. Evolution is not just about origins, but also about continual development and the results of that development. That is, creation has not achieved its goal, but it strives towards a future fulfillment. We get a glimpse of this in the eighth chapter of St. Paul's letter to the Romans:

I consider that the sufferings of this present time are not worth comparing with the glory about to be revealed to us. For the creation waits with eager longing for the revealing of the children of God; for the creation was subjected to futility, not of its own will but by the will of the one who subjected it, in hope that the creation itself will be set free from its bondage to decay and will obtain the freedom of the glory of the children of God. We know that the whole creation has been groaning in labor pains until now; and not only the creation, but we ourselves, who have the first fruits of the Spirit, groan inwardly while we wait for adoption, the redemption of our bodies. For in hope we were saved. Now hope that is seen is not hope. For who hopes for what is seen? But if we hope for what we do not see, we wait for it in patience.

An evolutionary view of the cosmos encourages us and enables us to locate our hope of fulfillment and redemption not separated from the rest of creation, but along with all of creation. In the evolutionary principle that all things have a common ancestry, we come to realize

that we are all in this together. Certainly this is the Biblical view of redemption.

One of the more disturbing aspects of evolution is that it unavoidably involves so much suffering. For many sensitive people, this is what proves the nonexistence of God; for if there is a God and this God is all-powerful and all-loving, why would this God create a system in which living creatures prey on other living creatures, a system in which the weak have no chance of survival? Let me offer the following as a partial—and I must stress partial—answer.

Think of an adolescent experimenting with independence, trying to discover identity and personal goals. It is a rough transition from adolescence into adulthood, involving failed experiments as well as successful attempts at personal maturing and growth. Wise parents and teachers know that sometimes it is best not to interfere, but to let the failures happen so that one might possibly learn from such failures. This can be painful, both for the adolescents and for those responsible for their upbringing.

I would describe the universe to be in the same situation as an adolescent. It is still developing, and part of that developing involves experimenting with growth and independence through such means as natural selection. That which doesn't work, particularly in regard to the continuing development of life, is discarded, and that which enables life to continue is saved. It is not by any stretch of the imagination a smooth operation. But we do see that creation has learned from its experiments, that is, survival is not a matter of the survival of the fittest, but of cooperation. The strong cannot survive without the weak. Nature tends towards balance and equilibrium, otherwise the food chain collapses.

Continuing the analogy, in an evolutionary context God gives creation time and space to grow and mature, that it may be a free and independent creation, capable of choosing of its own free will to return the love offered to it by God. Please understand that in humankind creation has achieved the consciousness and rationality that enables it to make such a decision. But consciousness and rationality are relatively recent developments in the history of creation, being mere thousands of years old compared to the several billion years of the known universe.

And, as the Scriptures so graphically remind us, our consciousness tends towards rebelliousness (hence my analogy of adolescence).

Yet it is not as if God has left us on our own, to fend for ourselves. In the incarnation of God the Son as Jesus, we see that God has always been intimately involved in creation. Jesus is just as much a product of evolution as we are. Such an assertion is unavoidable if we are to take the full humanity of Jesus seriously. It is not as if God were outside of creation, inserting himself into it, forcing his will onto the material world. No, it is more a matter of God's having the humility and compassion to share in the experience of evolution with us.

We must remember that for Christians, the primary image of God given to us is not that of some all-powerful superbeing capable of achieving its whims, but rather it is the image of a humble and defenseless love presented to us in the suffering and death of Jesus on the cross. The best expression of this is the hymn quoted by St. Paul in the second chapter of Philippians:

Though he was in the form of God,
Jesus Christ did not regard equality with God
as something to be exploited,
but emptied himself,
taking the form of a slave,
being born in human likeness.
And being found in human form,
he humbled himself
and became obedient to the point of death—
even death on a cross.

The Christian revelation is that God is self-giving love. It is not that God is loving in his actions (although God is that), but that God's very being, God's very essence, is love. If that is the case, then anything that has existed, does exist, and will exist does so because there is love. Love is creative, and desires to be loved. However much love wants to be loved, though, it does not force itself onto its beloved. It desires to be loved freely. So it provides room for the beloved to grow and to be persuaded into a loving union with it.

The hymn quoted from Philippians shows us, I believe, not a God of power coercively forcing creation to conform to his will, but a God who tries lovingly to persuade us and encourage us to become more loving ourselves. The humble, defenseless love revealed in the suffering and death of Jesus shows us that it is only in such an offering of compassion that evil can truly be disarmed. It is in this way that God is shown to be all-loving and all-powerful.

For a fuller exposition on evolution and theology, let me encourage interested readers to read God After Darwin: A Theology of Evolution by John F. Haught, printed by the Westview Press. M.D.

The Strength of Compassion

By Br. Abraham

From the Fall 2002 Abbey Letter

We are blessed with a good library here at St. Gregory's, and the monks and guests take full advantage of the accumulated knowledge and wisdom found in our 11,000 volumes. One result of the studying I have done here is the realization that a valuable tool in reading is the ability to disagree courteously with the author on some points while still gleaning helpful information. With that in mind, one of my regular reading projects involves picking a different school of philosophy or an individual philosopher each spring and reading representative works of that school or individual. Many of the varied works from different historical eras that I have read have been helpful, and I go back to muse on them at times. One particular school that has caught my interest is the Stoics, founded in Athens a few generations after Socrates, and named after the porch *(stoa)* where they met and taught. My interest in these ancient Stoics led me to do some research with the computer, and on the Internet I found a number of works from living Stoics dealing with current issues. In fact, there is a thriving modern Stoa now using the Internet as its porch for meeting and discussions emphasizing ethical behavior, positive political activity, and self-control.

One Internet essay I read while visiting a Stoic Web site was from an author expressing her opinion of Christianity as weak because of its call for compassion. Although I respected her honest opinion, I thought that I should disagree with her on that matter. We corresponded, and in the process I realized how little I actually knew about compassion. After reading different opinions on the subject, and praying for guidance, I hammered out a view of compassion that goes something like this: compassion involves acknowledging that we would be like others and act like them if we found ourselves in the same situation (or more likely, that we would act worse than they if we found ourselves in the same situation), and so feeling their pains, fears, and joys with them, yet never excusing their wrongdoings. This is not the best definition, but it works for me right now. One aspect of this understanding of compassion is the point that even though we recognize why we and other people do some of the wrong things that we do, we still expect ourselves and others to grow out of any bad actions caused by those situations. In other words, we don't expect anyone, including ourselves, to be perfect, but we do desire everyone to grow.

We want them to grow because we love them, respect them, and recognize them as the beautiful children of God that they are, and *we* want them to reach their full potential. In that way, compassion can never be confused with codependency or condemnation, both of which are weak because they despair of ever growing out of childish behavior into the maturity that we all seek. Codependency is weak because it passively excuses and hides wrong behavior, and so misses opportunities to change that behavior. Condemnation is weak because it does not have the strength to envision future growth and work toward it, and so opts for the quick solution of judging and passing sentence. Compassion, on the other hand, is strong because it looks to the future with hope, offering encouragement and help to grow out of our infantile behavior, knowing that it will take a lot of time and energy to do so. It requires us to be diligent in observing our own behavior and to offer help and encouragement to others while not belittling either them or ourselves. It also requires that we never excuse any wrongdoing or shy away from the consequences, even as we forgive and are forgiven. Doing all of that takes strength.

One important source of strength that can enable us to practice compassion is humility. We don't often think of humility in the context

of strength, but true humility both requires and bestows strength. Humility involves seeing ourselves in truth, and the truth is: We are unique individuals created to live joyfully and peacefully with all other creatures. We are children of God who are growing into maturity. As we grow, we make mistakes, hurting ourselves and others, but we must not be so afraid of growth that we stagnate. We must also never make the mistake of pretending that we are already fully mature, and that others are beneath us in their level of growth. Humbly admitting that we are all equally in need of growth requires strength, because it forces us to deflate our egos and to admit that we are made of the same stuff as everyone else, and that we are just as capable of good and bad as they are. After doing that, we then gain the strength needed for compassion, because we are relieved of the heavy burden of perfection and given the easy yoke of progress.

Strengthened by humility, we can see the most notorious terrorists, warmongers, abusers, and corrupt business and government executives as fellow children of God who have been shaped by events and people in their past into our hurting brothers and sisters who are trapped in fear, hatred, and pain. With compassion, we can see ourselves in their place and ask if we would do any better than they. In fact, we are in their situation, because as Jesus tells us in the Sermon on the Mount, anyone who has ever harbored anger toward someone is liable to judgment, and anyone who has lusted for someone has already committed adultery in the heart. In addition to that, we should see ourselves in their place because they are fellow humans and part of our family. They deserve our compassion as siblings who have met with danger on the road to fulfillment as God's children. Yet, having said that, we must remember that since they do share that high status as divine offspring, we must never debase them by excusing their actions and allowing them to continue in their destructive behavior. In that light, justice must always be dealt with compassion instead of vengeance, and so should work to solve problems, not to lash out in anger. Compassion thus requires the strength of objectivity and self-control.

In some ways, having compassion on infamous criminals is easier than having compassion on our own family members and colleagues, because their much smaller faults are with us every day, grating on our nerves and causing grudges to grow. Practicing compassion on our closest neighbors and house mates requires strong humility because it forces us to admit that we do things that drive them crazy just as we have been annoyed by the things they do. Like the story in the gospel, we worry about the speck in someone else's eye while being slowly killed by a log of the same stuff in our own. It also takes strength and humility to admit that even though we drive others just as crazy as they drive us, they love and accept us anyway. Realizing this great compassion that others have for us is humbling indeed. It is true that everyone should be expected to practice common courtesy and follow standards of decent behavior, but holding grudges because of others' minor idiosyncrasies is not a fulfillment of that expectation. We must be strong enough to let go of the grudges, or they will wear us down into whiny, nagging harpies, preventing us from becoming the loving souls that we are created to be. Therefore, while requiring great strength, compassion also strengthens our true selves, rather than weakening us or being a sign of weakness.

Since compassion requires us to put ourselves in others' places, and since no one can ever fully know or understand the story of anyone else's situation and past (we would need to live their entire lives in order to do that), we can never fully practice true compassion. Only God knows everyone's complete story, and so in order to be fully compassionate we have to rely on God's compassion to flow through us. If we mean it as Christians when we say that Jesus is fully God and fully human, then we can be assured that God has compassion for us, because that means that God knows firsthand all the aspects of human life. The fully human Jesus experienced the complete range of human life from birth to death, including all those human desires and urges that we don't always like to admit. The fully divine Jesus knows human life, and therefore Divinity has complete compassion for Humanity, because God knows our story as one of us. God chooses the path of compassion, not the path of condemnation, because the incarnation of God in Jesus is a stamp of approval on human life, not a condemnation of it. God chooses the path of compassion, not the path of codependency, because even though he is almighty and all merciful, God does not always shield us from the consequences of our actions as free individuals.

It is good to remember that God is compassionate, because one of the most difficult areas of compassion involves having it for ourselves. We all know how often we harm ourselves and others through common faults such as holding grudges, gossiping, lying, and judging others. Sometimes we do even worse things. After realizing what we have done, many times we choose either to ignore our faults or to damn ourselves mercilessly, both actions only making things worse. We don't have to do either one of those destructive things. We can choose to have compassion on ourselves and therefore make things better. In order to do so, we must never let our wrongdoings go unheeded and unchallenged, nor must we condemn ourselves as unworthy of life or love. Instead, we must maturely admit our mistakes and bear the consequences of our actions, while taking the responsibility to repair as best we can the damage that we have caused. All of that takes a lot of strength, but our dignity as humans gives us that strength, aided by our compassionate God.

My understanding of compassion is not complete, and probably never will be. Even after learning about compassion I don't always practice it as I should. It isn't easy for most people, but our job is to grow, not to be immediately perfect, and so every time we do open our hearts in loving compassion, it is a step on the right path. May we be grateful for all those who have gone before us, prodding us in the right direction, leaving their vast knowledge and wisdom in our library so that we can learn from their successes and failures. May we also be grateful for those people currently publishing their ideas in new books and Internet Websites, such as the present-day Stoic philosopher who unwittingly informed me of my lack of compassion. She knows who she is and even though I still think she is wrong about compassion being a sign of weakness, I thank her, along with all the others whom God has given us as brothers and sisters in our life together, searching for ways to live more peacefully and joyfully in our wonderful world. Thank you all for sharing your strength.

If You Get There Before I Do

By Fr. William

From the Fall 2007 Abbey Letter

Perhaps you've seen pictures taken at a monastic profession that look like someone is lying on the floor, playing dead in a big way, covered by a funeral pall and surrounded by funeral candlesticks. You're not misinterpreting the picture. That part of the service is exactly what it looks like, and it is meant to be a reminder that the monk or nun must die to the world in order to live to Christ.

It is also a vivid memorial of what was actually going on when we were baptized into the death and resurrection of Jesus. And monastic profession (as the preacher at that service probably pointed out several times) is a particular way of living out the spiritual reality of our Baptism. For Christians, life and death are intimately intertwined, and Christ leads us through both on our way to God in Him.

Furthermore in the Communion of Saints, living and dead Christians are closely bound together in the body of Christ. We are one church, one family. In the monastery, this closeness between the living and the dead is especially obvious at the time of a monk's death. Like rites of passage everywhere, that's a time when formal religious ceremonies mingle with the personal and family ways of doing things in a way that is comforting and most holy.

Some monasteries are very old fashioned and bury their brethren

147

without embalming. That means (especially if their summers are as hot as ours) that they bury their brethren quite soon after death. Here, we want the members of the departed monk's family to be able to join us for the funeral. So that in turn means he will be embalmed, to help through the wait while his friends and family come to say goodbye.

Once the embalming is taken care of, our brother's mortal remains are dressed in his monastic habit and laid out in a very plain wooden coffin with rope handles, made by the monastery's maintenance man. Then he comes back to the Abbey church for the last time. His coffin waits in the church for the funeral mass, covered by the pall and surrounded by the candlesticks that covered and surrounded him at his life profession.

I feel the closeness between the living and the dead especially during this time. Every time we go to church, we are also visiting our brother, paying our respects to one of our own who has gone before us into the next world. And whenever we want to take time for a personal visit and time by the coffin, the church is just a few minute's walk from wherever we are on the monastery grounds.

Then when the family and friends have arrived, we offer the funeral mass. It's one of those family times—I mean the monastic family here—when our father, the Abbot, is the celebrant and preacher. As the coffin and the congregation leave the church, the tower bell begins tolling, and continues to ring, slowly, solemnly, all through the graveside service.

And now the realities of country life kick in. The monastery has its own burial ground. But it's a bit too far and a bit too uphill for folks to walk carrying a coffin in a seemly manner. So the deceased gets to ride. Just what he rides depends on the condition of the dirt road to the cemetery. When conditions are good, then he goes all uptown and gets to ride in a hearse. But if the road is a mess, then he'll ride like the country boy he was, in the back of a truck or maybe in a wagon pulled by a tractor.

When we're all at the cemetery, monks and friends lay the coffin on the two-by-fours that span the open grave for the Committal service. Once those prayers have been offered, some of us tie ropes to the handles, and lift the coffin a few inches, while others remove

the two-by-fours so we can lower the monk's remains into their last resting place. And then we pick up our shovels and fill in the grave. This is a great comfort for us: this act of personally, physically, burying our departed members. And the guests usually want to share in that work as well, in spite of being in their dressy funeral clothes. The congregation tends to disperse as folks walk away after they have taken a turn with the shovels. So at the end there are just a final few adding the last shovels of dirt to the mound over the grave. Those folks will sometimes finish with an impromptu favorite prayer or song of the deceased before heading back downhill to the monastery.

It's not an unusual thing for a rural church in this part of the country to have its own graveyard on the grounds. But we monks have a particular advantage in keeping close to those who have gone before us. After all, we live at church. And so the closeness between the living and the dead isn't just a spiritual reality for us; it's a physical one as well. We can visit the graves of our departed brothers as frequently as we wish. We don't have to drive to church, we just have to go outside and walk up the hill.

We can visit the cemetery anytime, and so we do. But there's a day that's especially appropriate for all the members of the church to take the trouble to visit the graves of those we love who are no longer with us. That is November 2nd, All Souls' Day, an observance begun in the tenth century by the Benedictine monks of Cluny. It's a day set aside to show affection and reverence for our dead. We remember them and what they were to us, we give thanks for the benefits we received from them and pray that they may grow in their knowledge and love of God. And we can give alms in their memory. (It's funny, we think of memorial gifts at the time a friend dies; but so often we forget that we can aid the needy in memory of a departed friend at any time. After all it's an ancient and commendable act of Christian piety to do so.)

But one day a year isn't very much. Even two days a year aren't much—we Benedictines keep a day for All Souls of Our Order later in November. In fact, popular devotion has made the entire month of November a time to keep our beloved dead in mind. So on many November mornings I'll be in our cemetery, saying my prayers and sprinkling holy water on the graves. Doing this helps keep fresh the bonds of affection that tie me to those who lie there, the folks who were significant parts of my life, and the folks I never knew.

Maybe you'll join me. Not here, I mean. But perhaps your church has a graveyard or a columbarium on the property. Allow a bit of time, when you go to church in November, to pay a visit and say a prayer for those there who sleep in Jesus. And if you can't visit the graves of those particularly dear to you, November can still be a time to go through old photographs and souvenirs from days gone by. But this time as you look at your pictures and handle your souvenirs, do it with a prayer on your lips.

And we also bless thy holy Name for all thy servants departed this life in thy faith and fear, beseeching thee to grant them continual growth in thy love and service; and to grant us grace so to follow the good examples of all thy saints, that with them we may be partakers of thy heavenly kingdom.

Part Four:

EASTER

Darkness & Light

By Prior Aelred

From the Easter 2006 Abbey Letter

The literary critics say that in his plays, Shakespeare frequently followed his tragic scenes with humorous ones. They say that the contrast makes the serious seem more tragic and the comic more humorous. I don't know if any of that is true; it never seemed to please English teachers or creative writing professors when I tried it, but it is interesting that in the Church's traditional celebration of the mystery of Easter she juxtaposes darkness and light as images of our dark and sinful need for the glorious light of Christ.

In the course of three days we participate in the greatest of cosmic dramas, moving from the celebration of the institution of the Blessed Sacrament, to the lynching of the Messiah by nailing him to the cross, through the longest day of waiting, to the glorious triumph of the saving love of the resurrection that blessed, intimate touch, "Mary!", "Rabbouni!"

Sin has done its utmost. The divine response was healing through a forgiving love that conquered sin, death and darkness, and will conquer us, too, if only we will let it. Because we see here not only the contrast of light and darkness, but the contrast of time and eternity transitory time and immediate presence of eternity. Because we really see it, we are not just going through the motions of remembering past events that we have been told about by others; we are witnesses of these things. More than that, we are participants. We are involved because it is our own sins that are put to death and it is we ourselves who are raised to life.

This is not a repetition of Calvary that we playact each year; there is only one death and rising. No, these events transcend time and are always present in God's eternal now. As we move through these events, we are privileged to share in that now. Momentarily we move from time to taste eternity, from *chronos* to *kairos*. According to Dom Gregory Dix, this is true of every Eucharist, but Christ's resurrection is the living inception of our faith.

At St. Gregory's we don't use the Apostle's Creed in the Divine Office, but I ask you to remember the words from the Prayer Book Office, "He descended to the dead." (For those of us who better remember the words of the 1928 Prayer Book it was, "He descended into hell." The wording is different, but in spite of the complaints of the disaffected, the Church is not claiming that the truth has changed, but it does acknowledge that the meaning of words does change. "Hell" once meant "Sheol, or Hades," which simply meant the place where the dead people were. It did not mean the hell of eternal damnation. It meant the place where Christ descended to bring all of humanity into his glorious kingdom, as recounted in the First Letter of St. Peter

In John's Gospel we read that God enlightens everyone who comes into the world. When that light is heeded, when people try to do the best they can with what they have (as Erasmus would have put it), their life has integrity that is completed by Christ's coming to them to rescue them from the dark powers of the evil one. The icon is called, "The Harrowing of Hell." The words may have changed their meanings, but the truth that is expressed is that God is claiming Satan's victims for himself, both now and for ever. This is a most beautiful truth where time is lost in eternity, as darkness is overwhelmed by light, and sin and death overcome in the merciful redeeming love of our Savior who has risen from the dead to save us for ever and ever.

The God of the Living

By Abbot Andrew

From the Easter 2003 Abbey Letter

In St. Luke's account of the Resurrection, the women who come to the tomb to anoint the body of Jesus do not find the body they were looking for. Instead, they meet two young men in dazzling clothes who ask them: "Why do you look for the living among the dead?" This question suggests that it is illogical to go to a tomb in search of a live person. The women, however, were not being illogical. They were looking for a corpse, and the tomb where the body was laid was the place to look for it. The deeper suggestion of this question, of course, is that the women were looking for the wrong thing. They were looking for a corpse to anoint when they should have been looking for a live person to celebrate. This question of these two young men in dazzling clothes is foreshadowed by Jesus' assertion that the God of Abraham, Isaac and Jacob is God not of the dead but of the living. Anybody who seeks the dead rather than the living is fundamentally mistaken.

Even so, we should not overlook the fact that the women's action was not only logical but natural. The violent death of a loved one had occurred. Grief and anger over the unjust suffering and death of Jesus coupled by a desire to give dignity to an undignified death are natural. Since they thought, with good reason, that Jesus was dead, the women came to the tomb looking for him. Just as natural was the

action of Jesus' disciples: They ran and hid. Although the women were mistaken in looking in a tomb for Jesus, they were less mistaken than the disciples who were not looking for Jesus anywhere. By facing the reality of Jesus' death and coming to do the one constructive thing they could do in the face of that death, the women were challenged to let go of their grief and anger and embrace the life of the one who was not in the tomb after all. It is indeed outside the tomb where Jesus is found among the living.

We, too, are challenged by the question posed to the women: Do we look for the living among the dead? As long as we are stuck at Jesus' death, we are trapped in the grief and anger this death causes us to feel and we feel as if we, too, were dead. If we move on to the life of Jesus, then our grief and anger are engulfed in Jesus' abundant life and we feel very much alive, knowing, deep in our hearts, that God is God not of the dead, but of the living.

Easter Day Homily 2007
By Prior Aelred

From the Easter 2008 Abbey Letter

One of the curious things about the Gospel accounts of the risen Jesus is that when people who knew him before his crucifixion see him after his Resurrection, they do not recognize him. They don't seem to be afraid; they don't react as so many people in Jewish Scriptures do when they encounter an angel of the Lord, expecting to drop dead. They recognize Jesus as a human being, they just don't recognize him as Jesus.

We could come up with all kinds of theories as to why Mary Magdalene doesn't recognize Jesus as he stands before her in the garden as told in John's Gospel. She is obviously deeply upset, her eyes full of tears, and her imagination full of fears of death and grave-robbers. She is so single-minded in her search for the dead body of her Lord, that even a meeting with a pair of angels becomes uninteresting unless they can give her the one piece of information she wants.

But none of these seem convincing explanations of why she doesn't recognize Jesus. This is a woman whose whole mind is full of the man who is standing right in front of her, and yet she does not know him. The simple explanation must be the true one—that real life is something we don't understand very well without divine aid. In this case, Jesus gives Mary Magdalene the ability to see by using a word. He says her name, and allows her to see who he is, and to connect the old life she used to know with the new life that now stands before her.

Let me suggest something that will sound odd—life is not natural. Life is God's free gift. God loves us into existence. We would not continue to exist without the ongoing and continuous love that God wants to share with us.

We have always before us the reminder of the risen Lord. We need this to help us to recognize God's life when it appears in our own lives. The Lord's voice calls us by name, so that, like the Magdalene, we suddenly look up and recognize the Lord of life standing in front of us.

But our lives don't stop. Like Mary Magdalene, we have to return to our former life, but somehow seeing that while it is still the same, it is also profoundly changed by the new resurrected life of our Lord that he wants to share with us.

We are told not to cling to Jesus, as much as we might want to do precisely that. Instead, we are told to go to others to tell them what we have experienced, continuing to seek him in the unexpected places or among the unexpected people in a mystery, as Colossians puts it, "...hidden with Christ in God," to tell everyone about the transforming love of God made visible in Christ Jesus our Lord.

Saved by the Life of Jesus

By Abbot Andrew

From the Easter 2010 Abbey Letter

Once upon a time there was a powerful king who owned all the land in the world. In the beginning, the king had given his servants everything they needed to tend the land so that it would bear fruit. But the servants failed to produce as much fruit as they should have, so that even from the beginning, all of them were in debt to the king. These debts could not possibly have been paid even if all of the servants put their hearts and souls into farming the land. The servants became discouraged and farmed less and less while their debts grew and grew. The king was dismayed over this growing debt and the growing failure of all his servants to give him the produce and the honor that was his due. Since it was clear that the servants would never be able to pay what they owed the king, the king decided that the only way to restore justice was to do away with all his servants. When the king told his son what he had resolved to do, the king's son, who loved the servants, suggested that since he owed no debt, he could give his life for all of the servants and the debt would be paid. The king didn't want to lose his son, but he didn't want to lose all of his servants either, so finally he agreed to his son's suggestion and ordered his servants to put his son to death. Thus the debt was paid and all the servants lived happily ever after.

Does this story disturb you? It disturbs me. What disturbs me most about this story is that the king cannot or will not forgive the debt and will *only* be satisfied if somebody pays the debt, even if it is the king's innocent son who pays it. If we take this story to be a parable about God and our redemption in Christ, we have a troubling portrait of God who, in effect, requires that his son be a sacrifice to *him*.

The notion that God sent his son to die as a sacrifice to him attempted to solve a problem in a teaching in the early church that suggested that the devil had gained the rights over humanity because of our fall into sin, and God came to our rescue by bargaining with the devil to redeem us. In this scheme, God gave his Son in exchange for us, but the injustice of killing God's Son caused the devil to forfeit his rights over humanity. An analogy commonly used was that the man Jesus was the bait to tempt the devil and Jesus' divinity was the hook that caught the devil. The humor of this model of redemption is refreshing compared to the dour situation of Jesus being a sacrifice to his own Father, but the notion that God had to bargain with the devil is a big problem. Unfortunately, taking the devil out of the equation left only the king and his son so that all the bargaining was between the king (God) and the king's son (Jesus). Recently, some theologians have complained that this theological model portrays God as a child abuser. If God is the greatest good of all, then surely we can come up with a better model of redemption than this.

I once had a theology professor who explained how theologians such as St. Augustine thought that God had gotten into a pickle over what he called "God's dilemma over sin." God had to do something about the mess humanity had fallen into, but God couldn't just forgive the sin outright because that would be unjust. But Jesus' Parable of the Prodigal Son (better called the Parable of the Prodigal Father) cuts the Gordian knot of this dilemma with a decisive stroke. The father forgives his wayward son when his son is only trying to get a better meal than he got when he was feeding the pigs. Presumably, the older, obedient son would agree with theologians who posit this divine dilemma over sin. On the contrary, Jesus forgave the paralytic his sins before healing him, and Jesus inaugurated his teaching ministry at Capernaum by declaring the year of the Lord's favor. The Jubilee, as it was called in Leviticus, is a fresh start for all when all debts are forgiven. This makes it highly unlikely that God required Jesus' blood in order to forgive us our sins.

Jesus' parable of the evil workers in the vineyard also gives us a very different picture than the story of the king who sent his son to be a sacrifice to himself. Here, the death of the owner's son was in no way willed by the owner; it was willed by the workers. In this grim parable, Jesus is warning us that we will enact the same violence against him unless we repent. In the Gospel narratives of Jesus' death, neither God nor the devil killed Jesus. Human beings did it, and we know the names of some of them. Jesus' death in these narratives is not portrayed as a divine necessity, but a *human* necessity for people like Pontius Pilate, Caiaphas, and the rest of us.

If God does not really need Jesus' blood in order to redeem us, if Jesus' death is *not* the vehicle of our redemption, then what is? The answer is: Jesus' *Life*. If all we had were Jesus' death, then the most we would have would be the inspiration that the self-sacrifice of an

innocent person gives us and the lesson this judicial murder teaches us about our propensity to scapegoating violence. But chances are we wouldn't even have that if Jesus' death was the end of the story. Jesus' death left his few remaining followers scattered and demoralized. It was his risen life that reunited them with Jesus so that they could tell the story that has come down to us, and his risen life unites us to him as well.

The theologian Raymund Schwager, in discussing the parable of the evil workers, notes that Jesus did not fulfill the threat implied by the rhetorical question that ends the parable of the evil workers in the vineyard. Jesus did not tear Pontius Pilate and Caiaphas to pieces. What Jesus did was continue to do the same thing he was doing when he was killed, which was to gather all of us together to a new way of living, free of the collective violence that killed Jesus and countless victims, before and since. By gathering Paul into the nascent church, Jesus made it clear that he believed what he preached about loving his enemies. The parable of the two brothers and their prodigal father also makes it clear that God responds with love and forgiveness to those who stray.

Suggesting that the Resurrection is the vehicle of our redemption doesn't deny the significance of Jesus' death, but the Gospel record and the apostolic preaching in Acts suggest that Jesus' death says a lot more about human beings than it does about God. Jesus' death makes it clear that if humans choose to respond to God's call with violence, then God will suffer that violence. Jesus said that he came to give life and to give it abundantly. That means Jesus did not come to die; he came to give life, and Jesus' death could not stop him from doing that. We can speak of Jesus' death on the cross as part of God's plan, as Peter does in his first sermon, but Peter links this plan to God's foreknowledge, which is very different from God's will. Peter says that it is we humans who crucified and killed Christ by the hands of those outside the law. God didn't do it. What *did* God do? God raised Jesus up, having freed him from death, because it was impossible for him to be held in its power.

The story of Jesus' Resurrection has not come to an end. The story spills out of the New Testament into our lives with its challenge to let God gather us into the abundant life God offers us. We may think God is being soft by making this offer even to the worst of criminals, but God's magnanimous offer of abundant life poses a huge challenge to us because it exposes the element of death in many of the things we do and think. We will find out very quickly that we will have to die to all of that before we can receive God's life to the full. In the house of the Prodigal Father, there is room for neither a wasted lifestyle nor self-righteous sulking. Jesus did not end this parable about the two brothers. Like the Gospel, it flows out of the pages into our lives, leaving it for us to decide if we will accept the invitation to dwell forever in the Prodigal Father's House.

Christ Shall Give You Light
By Fr. William

From the Easter 2001 Abbey Letter

At the life profession of a monk of St. Gregory's Abbey, the monk makes his vows at the offertory of the Mass, and leaves a signed, handwritten copy of those vows on God's altar. Then he lies prostrate on the floor of the choir, in the place where his coffin will someday rest during his funeral. He is covered with the funeral pall, the cloth that will on that day drape his coffin, and the other monks and the congregation chant the litany of the saints over him. At the end of the prayers, the deacon comes to the edge of the pall and says, "Awake you who sleep, and arise from the dead, and Christ shall give you light."

The inclusion of a funeral rite in the service of monastic consecration is not an exclusively Christian practice. Hindus, for instance, do it too. But for Christian monastics it has a particular meaning not found in other faiths. It is a way of reenacting our baptism. And our baptism is the Church's, and God's, way of uniting us with the saving death of Jesus Christ. As St. Paul writes to the Romans, "Do you not know that all of us who have been baptized into Christ Jesus were baptized into his death? Therefore we have been buried with him by baptism into death, so that, just as Christ was raised from the dead by the glory of the Father, so we too might walk in newness of life."

There are many differences between God's becoming human in

order to share our life and death, and our going under the water to share the death and new life of God incarnate. To begin with, God is the creator of life. The generations of human beings who have given birth to generations of human beings have all been passing on a gift that they received from those who came before. But the Word of God who was born of Mary was the original maker and giver of that gift. The opening of the Gospel according to St. John tells us, "All things came into being through him, and without him not one thing came into being. What has come into being in him was life, and the life was the light of all people. The light shines in the darkness, and the darkness did not overcome it."

When we read the story of this creation in Genesis, we find that God created the heavens and the earth and all that is in them, and rested on the seventh day. And that rest is not presented as a threatening thing, as the Creator's turning away from his work to tend to his own needs, nor as a withdrawing from interest and involvement in his creatures. It is seen as a good, if mysterious thing, and is celebrated in the command for Israel to observe every seventh day as a day of rest in remembrance of the Lord's rest and as a sharing in it.

Things appear different when Jesus cries from the cross, "It is finished!" and closes his eyes in the last sleep of mortals. It is a sad and ugly thing to see him on the cross. And perhaps less ugly but more sad to see him laid in the tomb. But there in his borrowed tomb, the Creator picks up where we left him at the seventh day of the creation story: at rest. While his mortal body rests in death, he creates life, his life and ours, anew. His resurrection body, living this new life, is the first dawning of the new heaven and the new earth that are to come.

This triumph of life over death, of light over darkness, is the message the Easter sunrise proclaims to us year after year. It is what we sing about in our Easter hymns, so full of joy and glory:

That Easter day with joy was bright, the sun shone out with
fairer light ...
Welcome, happy morning!' age to age shall say ...
Christ himself the joy of all, the sun that warms and lights us;
by his grace he doth impart eternal sunshine to the heart ...

*Come, with high and holy hymning, hail our Lord's triumphant
day; not one darksome cloud is dimming yonder glorious
morning ray, breaking o'er the purple east, symbol of our Easter
feast....*

And symbol of our Easter feast it is. The rising sun's light and
warmth, driving out the darkness and chill of the night, provide a
natural and powerful sign of Christ's victory over sin and death. So
it makes sense that we find a sunrise on Easter cards and in the last
scene of Easter pageants, as well as in the hymns we sing. It makes
sense for churches and communities to meet for a sunrise service on
Easter morning.

But the Prayer Book also gives us a service for the night before that
sunrise. In the Easter Vigil, we gather to worship in that darker time
when the sunrise victory was actually won. We gather, as it were, on
the battleground where life fought against darkness and death and the
Devil, and fought them on their own turf. We gather to read the Old
Testament stories and prophecies of the struggle between darkness and
light, life and death. We listen to the deacon chant in a church dimly
lit by candlelight, "How holy is this night, when wickedness is put to
flight, and sin is washed away...How blessed is this night, when earth

and heaven are joined and man is reconciled to God." And before we begin the Eucharist, with its alleluias and bells and lively, joyful hymns, we recall our Baptism, renewing our vows and being sprinkled with holy water.

That night service reflects much of the truth of our life in this world. We live in the mixture of light and dark, of death and life, of good and evil. We who live in that condition are called the church militant. We are fighting, struggling for the victory of light, life, and goodness, both in our own personal lives and in our society. We are carrying on the divine works of creation and re-creation. We keep on doing the work God has given us to do until we enter our own Sabbath rest. And when that day comes, we can enter into our rest in confidence and hope because of the one who has gone before us:

My flesh in hope shall rest, and for a season slumber,
till trump from east to west shall wake the dead in number.
Had Christ that once was slain, ne'er burst his three-day prison,
our faith had been in vain; but now is Christ arisen.

They Discussed Among Themselves What Rising from the Dead Could Mean

By Prior Aelred

From the Easter 2004 Abbey Letter

It is so easy and so tempting to feel superior to the Twelve when we read St. Mark's Gospel. They never seem to understand what Jesus is getting at whereas we (who have the distinct advantage of knowing how things are going to turn out) do. Of course the author intended for the readers (and hearers) of the Gospel to feel this way. I always find it rather encouraging. If the Twelve could get things so wrong when they tried to follow Jesus, then there might be hope for me.

Only in the Marcan account of the Transfiguration are we told that Peter, James, and John discussed among themselves what rising from the dead could mean. Typically, commentators say that this indicates the inability of these three disciples to comprehend what the Son of Man rising from the dead could possibly have to do with Jesus, whom they had just witnessed in glory. I am sure that it is quite true that they had difficulty understanding the possibility of a suffering savior, but I also think that there is more to it than that. I think they wondered, as I do myself, what rising from the dead could mean.

It seems that many modern Christians who say they believe in the resurrection of the dead really think in terms of the continued spiritual existence of an immortal soul or some sort of continuation of the personality or continued individual consciousness. There might be some truth to these usually vague notions, but it stretches a metaphor pretty far to consider them to be rising from the dead.

Although I have had my moments of disagreement with the eminent New Testament scholar (and recently appointed Bishop of Durham) N. T. Wright, he is surely correct to point out that discussions of whether St. Paul was familiar with the Empty Tomb tradition are irrelevant. For a Jew of the first century, any understanding of our continued existence after death would have to involve an embodied life. God has clearly made us to be embodied and any other way of our living is difficult to imagine (which is doubtless why speculation about disembodied continuation of our existence is so vague). As the great liturgist, Dom Gregory Dix, observed, "the disembodied continuation of the immortal soul is not Christian but neo-Platonist." Now, I do not want to take cheap shots at Plato or Plotinus or St. Augustine or any other of the Fathers who were deeply influenced by neo-Platonic thought. It was the predominant world view of their time and if the Gospel is to be preached it must be preached in a way that can be understood (in spite of the risk of momentary misunderstanding or distortion—one must trust that the Holy Spirit will continue to act as a corrective). Nor would I suggest that the belief in the immortality of the soul is necessarily untrue, or that the mysterious resurrection body that St. Paul talks about requires continuity of the identical matter that constituted our bodies in this brief and transitory life (the body's regeneration and replacement of its own material was recognized at least as early as Aquinas, who worried about the implications of cannibalism for the resurrection body).

Nevertheless, there is a tendency in the Platonic view to assume that spiritual is by definition good (or higher) and physical or earthly is bad (or lower). This assumption struck me quite forcibly a few years ago when I read through the entire *Philokalia*. This collection of sayings from the monastic traditions of the Eastern Churches spans the period from the 4th century Desert Fathers (I particularly liked St. Mark the Hermit) to the 15th century monks of Mt. Athos. In the earliest sayings there is no disparagement of the corporeal but increasingly, the later entries equate the material with evil and the spiritual with good.

Also, as a sacramental Episcopalian, I remember being stunned by the comment of Ralph Waldo Emerson who said that he stopped celebrating the Lord's Supper because he believed that the spiritual could have nothing to do with the material. Emerson was a great genius, of course, who frequently could see the essence of a situation, as he did

regarding the sacraments. Unfortunately, it seems to me that in this case he got things exactly backwards. The material always involves the spiritual. We attempt to separate them at the risk of misunderstanding and misusing both.

We monks have the opportunity to reflect on this tendency when St. Gregory's has guests from various Protestant traditions worshiping with us. For whatever reasons (and I think they are rather complex and not all to be blamed on Plato) they seem to regard worship as exclusively a mental process and seat themselves on the chairs in the nave and remain fixed there throughout the service while the community engages in what the actor (and Episcopalian) Robin Williams describes as "pew aerobics." And at the time of the English Reformation, there were Puritans who strenuously objected to kneeling for Communion and insisted that the minister bring them the sacred elements while they remained seated in their pews—as is indeed the practice in the great majority of Protestant churches in this country to this day.

It would be incorrect to suggest that there is not some truth in this understanding of worship; our own monastic service of Matins reflects the descriptions of the early monastic services in Egypt described by St. John Cassian and involves little in the way of communal activity. For the most part we sit in the dark and listen as psalms and lessons are read—all very mental or spiritual.

But a cognitive or educational understanding of worship is at best partial. Another universal aspect of human worship, and one that the Early Church continued from its Jewish origins, has involved movement and song and incense and color and eating and drinking—involving not just the mental faculties but all the human senses that are involved in the embodiedness that was God's intention for us from our creation.

There is also a theological tension that might begin as early as the New Testament writings themselves between a Johanine emphasis on seeing (We shall become like him because we shall see him as he really is) and the more typical image expressed in the synoptic tradition of the Kingdom as a banquet. When Aquinas was trying to clarify the mysteries of the Christian faith he was quite puzzled to explain how the

Beatific Vision could be improved by the addition of a body following the General Resurrection.

I believe that we will be transformed by the Holy Spirit into the Christ whom we see with our unveiled faces, but I do not presume to know exactly what that entails. However, I do believe that it will involve our continued life in Christ in a way that fulfills the corporeal nature that God has willed for us in that heavenly banquet in which we hope to partake, through Christ our Lord.

Marantha!: Come Lord Jesus!
By Abbot Andrew

From the Easter 1999 Abbey Letter

The approach of the new millennium triggered so many prophecies of doom that we are inclined to think that we live in an apocalyptic age. Historians, however, remind us that the turn of the first millennium also set off much the same prophecies, except that there was less human technology to weave into these prophecies. Moreover, the historical record shows us that, far from waiting for the turn of a millennium to indulge in such speculations, humanity has created a steady stream of apocalyptic prophecies over at least the past three thousand years.

Within Christianity, expectations of the end of time are connected with the Second Coming of Christ. The combination of many impressively violent prophecies in the Bible and Jesus' promise to be with us until the end of time has helped lead many to visions of Jesus making a violent return to the earth to take care of evil people once and for all. The famous fresco of the Last Judgment by Michelangelo in the Sistine Chapel is the culmination of centuries of Christian art that illustrates the Second Coming of Jesus as wrathful and violent. Yearning for the coming of Christ is basic to Christian spirituality. Just before the benediction that closes the Bible, St. John the Divine joins St. Paul in crying out: "Maranatha! Come, Lord Jesus!" But do we really want to bring on stage a cosmic warrior who will fight the war that makes all other wars look like children playing with wooden swords? If we are to say the word Maranatha with all our heart, we had better do some thinking and praying about what kind of person we are asking for and what that person might be up to when he comes.

Since the passages in the Old Testament which portray God's threats to commit violence greatly outnumber the promises of divine acts of healing, and since the Jews in Jesus' time chafed under Roman rule, it is no wonder that they expected a violent Messiah who would destroy the Roman Empire on their behalf. John the Baptist seems to have shared the usual expectations generated by biblical prophecy when he castigated the evildoers for fleeing the wrath to come. On the contrary, Jesus didn't injure people for their sins, he healed them. He didn't cast out sinners, he sat at table with them. In contrast to the custom of sending a scapegoat out into the wilderness to die for the sins of the people, Jesus told the parable of the lost sheep that is brought home with rejoicing. Jesus' tirade against the Pharisees and his act of overthrowing the money changers' tables in the temple precincts are the closest things to violence on his part that we find in the Gospels, but it is noteworthy that Jesus, even then, with the people who seem to have exasperated him the most, did not turn the Pharisees into lepers or send fire down from Heaven on the heads of the money changers. Indeed, Jesus was quite selective as to which prophecies he was going to fulfill and which ones he would not. That is, he discerned which verses served as keys for the others. Jesus rode into Jerusalem on a donkey, an image of peace, when he could have ridden a horse, an image of war. Jesus told Pilate that he could have called on twelve legions of angels, but he didn't. Instead, Jesus allowed the Roman soldiers to lead him out of the city to be crucified in fulfillment of the prophecies of the suffering of Yahweh's Servant in Isaiah 40-55.

If Jesus could have called on twelve legions of angels to rout Pilate and the Pharisees in one fell swoop before his death, surely Jesus had a lot more power to throw around after rising from the dead. The risen Jesus could have had his revenge with interest against those who persecuted him. But Jesus did nothing of the kind. He appeared gently to his disciples and gathered back together the small frightened group of men and women who had followed him and then fled from the arrest, the cross, or the empty tomb. When Jesus appeared, he called his friends by name, said to the re-gathered group, "Peace be with you." There were no recriminations for their failing Jesus during his time of trial, although the three-fold question to Peter, "Do you love me?" seems to be a reparation for Peter's threefold denial in the courtyard of the high priest. On the road, he explained the scriptures to them while their hearts burned within them. In Galilee, Jesus gathered his followers, including those who doubted. Given the list of curses for infidelity to God in Deuteronomy 28, he let those who forsook him off pretty easy. Most important of all, Jesus breathed the Holy Spirit into his followers and admonished them to forgive sins. The Holy Spirit is called the Paraclete in John's Gospel; that is, he is the Advocate for the defense. Since the Holy Spirit is the Advocate of all people, we are not being given permission to bind the sins of others; we are being warned that if we don't use the breath of the Advocate to forgive, the sins will remain bound—to us! Given this data about Jesus, why is there so much expectation of a violent return on the part of Jesus?

One answer has to do with what we find in our hearts. Our sense of justice often causes us to yearn for a swift and violent end of those who perpetrate atrocities. Such desires are given powerful expression in some of the psalms, such as Psalm 58 where the righteous bathe their feet in the blood of the wicked. We hate it if we are sure that a criminal has gotten away scot-free because he could hire a good lawyer. Even worse, when an atrocious unsolved crime has been committed, it becomes difficult to live with that irresolution. Society is not comforted until somebody has been punished, no matter how flimsy the evidence for conviction might really be. However, Jesus made it clear in such parables as that of the laborers in the vineyard and the prodigal son that he knew well that we do not like it if other people get more from God than they deserve. But this vindictive attitude, for all its noble justice, is just not the attitude he wants to encourage in his followers. The cursing psalms mentioned above remind us that when severe suffering is inflicted upon us, forgiveness does not come easily. We may first need to join the martyrs who cry for vengeance from under the altar after the opening of the fifth seal in the sixth chapter of Revelation. The trouble is, as long as we bathe our feet in the blood of the wicked we cannot be washed in the Blood of the Lamb. The martyrs are given white robes and told to be patient, patient enough to join the huge number, impossible to count, who have been through the Great Persecution and who are too busy praising the Lamb to cry out for vengeance against their enemies.

A second answer is that the Biblical prophecies of violence seem to remain unfulfilled. Perhaps Jesus didn't fulfill those prophecies the first time around because he wanted to save some spectacular fireworks for the end of all time. The violent imagery in the Revelation of St. John the Divine fuels such speculations of a violent return of Jesus. The images of violence, however, are best understood through the central image in the heavenly scene of the Lamb of God who was slain, whose body still bears the marks of the violence suffered at human hands. Only the slain Lamb is deemed worthy to open the scroll and break its seven seals. One might be inclined to think that the visions of catastrophes that unfold when the scroll is opened by the Lamb portray a divine temper tantrum over human sinfulness. What is really happening is that Jesus is revealing the truth of human violence. In his death, Jesus revealed for all time the hidden truth that humans, insofar as we are separated from the true God, will solve social tensions of rivalry with each other through the act of scapegoating a victim. This is precisely the story told in the passion narratives of the Gospels. This is the violence that leads humanity to exacerbate natural disasters of famine and plague through economic greed and war. This is the violence that spins out of control when the slain lamb reveals the truth with his tongue that cuts like a two-edged sword. The truth is a word of peace, but to a human heart that retains violence, the truth, like a surgical wound, hurts before it heals.

In his apocalyptic discourses in the Gospels, all of the violence Jesus warns us about is committed through human agency. In the midst of the human chaos, Jesus, the Son of Man, appears on the clouds of heaven. What is the Son of Man doing? He is not bashing in the heads of the bad guys who made a mess of the world. Instead, he is gathering all who belong to him, and that is all he is doing. Jesus is showing us that he is the resurrection and the life and that is all he is. In his book *Raising Abel* James Alison writes, "God, being alive has nothing to do with death and cannot even be contrasted with death." Jesus does not come to bring death because his life has nothing to do with it. He comes only to bring life. Both the Sermon on the Mount and Jesus' suffering at the hands of humanity make it clear that violent responses to violence are simply not appropriate, either for God or for humans. Our fundamental choice is either to join God in gathering all people to Him, or to scatter ourselves and the rest of God's people to the ends of the earth. In revealing the truth about the violence in our hearts, Jesus also reveals the truth of the bountiful life we can live and share with all creation. The Prodigal Father invites both the wayward son and the dutiful son to the celebration. Will we come? Maranatha! Come, Lord Jesus!

CPSIA information can be obtained at www.ICGtesting.com
Printed in the USA
267114BV00001B/5/P